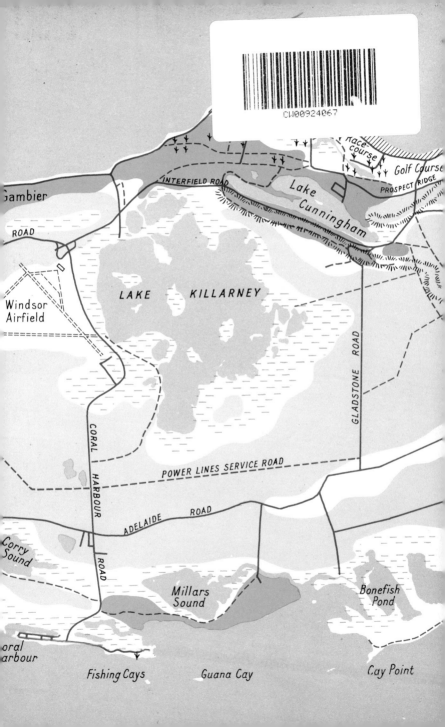

THE BIRDS OF NEW PROVIDENCE
AND THE BAHAMA ISLANDS

THE BIRDS OF
NEW PROVIDENCE
AND THE
BAHAMA ISLANDS

P. G. C. BRUDENELL-BRUCE

Illustrated by

HERMANN HEINZEL

COLLINS
St James's Place London
1975

ISBN 0 00 219030 3

© *P. G. C. Brudenell-Bruce, 1975*
Printed in Great Britain
Collins Clear-Type Press
London and Glasgow

CONTENTS

CONTENTS

PLATES

MAP OF
THE BAHAMA ISLANDS
Scale of Miles
0 10 20 40 60 80 100

N

FLORIDA

West Palm Beach
Fort Lauderdale
MIAMI

Matanilla Reef
Walkers Cay
Salex Cay
Spanish Cay
Green Turtle Cay
West End
Freeport
GREAT BAHAMA ISLAND
Marsh Harbour
Hope Town
The Marls
GREAT ABACO ISLAND
Sandy

NORTHWEST PROVIDENCE CHANNEL

Great Stirrup Cay
BERRY IS.
Frazers Hog Cay
Joulters Cays
NASSAU
NEW PROVIDENCE ISLAND

NORTHEAST PROVIDENCE CHANNEL

ATLANTIC

OCEAN

Harbour Is.
Governors Harbour
Palmetto Point
ELEUTHERA ISLAND
Tarpum Bay
Rock Sound
Cotton Bay

Highburn Cay
Norman Cay
Hawksbill Cay

BIMINI
Cat Cay

STRAITS OF FLORIDA

ANDROS ISLAND
Andros Town
TONGUE OF THE OCEAN
Big Wood Cay
Wood Cay

EXUMA SOUND

Arthurs Town
CAT ISLAND
The Bight
Moss Town

Fowl Cay
Great Guana Cay
Booby Rocks

Cockburn Town
SAN SALVADOR OR WATLINGS ISLAND

Water Cay
South Cay

GREAT EXUMA ISLAND
George Town
Little Exuma

RUM CAY

LONG ISLAND

GREAT BAHAMA BANK

SANTAREN CHANNEL

Sandy Cays
Jumento Cays
Flamingo Cay

Atwood or Samana Cay

CROOKED ISLAND PASSAGE

RAGGED ISLANDS
Seal Cay
Great Ragged Is.

CROOKED ISLAND

ACKLINS ISLAND

MAYAGUANA ISLAND

MAYAGUANA PASSAGE

CUBA

CAICOS PASSAGE

LITTLE INAGUA ISLAND

GREAT INAGUA ISLAND

Matthew Town

INTRODUCTION

The Bahama Islands consist of some seventeen sizeable islands, hundreds of smaller ones, and thousands of tiny cays and rocks, and extend some six hundred miles from north-west to south-east. They run from within fifty miles of the east coast of Florida to a similar distance from the eastern tip of Cuba, and occupy an immense sea area although their land surface is only 4,400 square miles. The Tropic of Cancer crosses rather more than half-way down the islands, traversing, to be exact, the bar of the Peace and Plenty Club in Georgetown, Exuma!

General Description and Climate

The islands are low-lying, and either swampy or covered with dense vegetation; this is mainly composed of coppice and scrub except on some of the northern islands where extensive pine forests grow. The introduced casuarina is common round settlements, but otherwise there are few large trees. There are lakes and ponds on most islands, some of them fresh, some salt, and some brackish; but even a fresh-water lake may rise and fall with the tide, its lower layers being salt water with egress to the sea. There are no streams or rivers with the exception of some sluggish channels on Andros.

The climate, except perhaps on the most southerly islands, is sub-tropical. The average day temperatures vary only about ten degrees between winter (approx. 21°C) and summer (approx. 27°C), but excessive humidity makes the summer climate somewhat disagreeable. The average rainfall is between forty-five and fifty inches, two-thirds of which falls between May and October, usually in brief, torrential downpours. The winds are usually south-easterly in summer (mere breezes in most places, but trade winds on the southern islands), and north-easterly in winter, when gales, known as 'northers', blow regularly for a day or two at a time. Hurricanes are a danger mainly from August to October; they come up from the south-east, but usually veer off into the Atlantic or the Gulf of Mexico.

Wildlife

The Bahama Islands are believed to have been covered by the sea for long periods, finally emerging about one million years ago, and all the forms of wildlife that now occupy them have had to come in from outside, from across the sea—a feat in which relatively few species have succeeded. In consequence there are rather few *resident* or native species of birds, and only one large mammal, the introduced racoon. Most of the resident birds are believed to have come from the West Indies rather than from Florida, the winds, sea-currents, and above all the hurricanes being favourable to immigration from the south or south-east. However a great many species of North American migrants pass through or spend the colder months in the islands, and they far outnumber the native birds during most of the year. More migrants pass south down the eastern coast of the US and through the Bahamas in autumn than return northwards in the spring, when the main migration route runs through central America and across the Gulf of Mexico.

NEW PROVIDENCE

New Providence lies in the northern half of the Bahamas, between Andros on the south-west, the Berry Islands on the north-west, Eleuthera on the east, and the Exuma chain on the south-east. This relatively central position and a sheltered harbour are, no doubt, the reasons why Nassau, the capital city, was sited on the island.

Overpopulation and its Effects

New Providence is by far the most heavily populated island in the Bahamas, for although it comprises only 1.3 per cent of the total land area it holds over 60 per cent of the human population. This naturally has an adverse effect on the bird life: a large part of the island is built-up, much natural habitat has been cleared for development, swamps have been drained and filled, and no part of the island is remote enough to allow larger birds, such as herons, to nest undisturbed.

But fortunately many compensating advantages derive from this over-population. There are, for instance, more gardens, more flowers, and more large deciduous trees, in the Nassau area than anywhere else in the Bahamas. These attract more birds, and probably more different species per acre, than are found in the wilder areas of coppice and pinewood. Naturally some species are unable to adjust themselves to living close to human beings, but there are many others that are either indifferent to it or actually benefit from it. Another feature of New Providence, as compared with the out islands, is the large amount of man-made open country, in the form of airfields, golf courses, and, to a lesser degree, sports grounds and cultivated areas. These increase the diversity of a countryside which in its natural form is entirely covered with vegetation.

General Description and Vegetation

New Providence is about twenty-one miles long by seven miles across at the widest point, a land area of some sixty square miles. Although one often wishes it were larger, it is, from the ornithologist's point of view, an almost ideal size: small enough for him to cover regularly and systematically, large enough to keep him busy. It is criss-crossed by roads and little-known tracks and paths.

The island is flat except for a low range of hills along the north; this becomes a double range on the eastern half of the island. Nassau stretches over a large part of the north-east, but there are only small settlements and sparsely populated developments elsewhere. The rest of the island falls into two main categories: the pine barrens, which cover most of the west end of the island and much of the south and centre; and coppice.

Both are curious forms of vegetation for both grow in profusion where, on the face of it, almost nothing should be able to live. This is particularly true of the pine barrens, where a dense growth of small pines provides shade for an equally flourishing growth of palms, palmetto, and undergrowth, all supported by the most inhospitable rock formation imaginable, the well-named 'honeycomb limestone'. This is, incidentally, extremely treacherous to walk on. Coppice tends to occupy less impoverished terrain, although it is a question of degree only on an island where earth is a commodity which is bought, sold, and carried about on trucks. It is probably no accident that coppice occupies the better ground, for a large part of the island grew crops in the days of slavery, and presumably the more favoured parts were chosen for this purpose. But with the freeing of the slaves farming became, and in general has remained, unprofitable, and the slave plantations quickly reverted to coppice. This is composed of trees and bushes of no great height, and is chiefly remarkable for its extraordinary density; for the most part it is literally impenetrable. It is divisible into 'high coppice' and 'low coppice', low coppice intergrading in turn with 'scrub', but the distinctions are arbitrary.

Mangroves and mangrove swamps also occupy a substantial part of the island. Mangroves grow only in salt or brackish water, and hold different species of birds according to whether they are in tidal marshes, as on the south side of the island, or in the brackish water of the smaller, inland marshes near the north coast. In general the brackish marshes are richest in bird life, although the brackish environs of Lake Killarney are particularly poor. There are a number of lakes, sounds, and ponds; Lake

Cunningham, where shooting is prohibited, is the most interesting of the larger sheets of water, but several of the smaller ponds are worth visiting. The sea coast is ornithologically poor along the north of the island, but quite rich on parts of the south coast, where muddy tidal flats predominate.

BIRD LIFE IN THE BAHAMAS

It is not possible to see as many different species of birds in the Bahamas as can be seen at certain times of the year in the USA, where one person can see 100, and exceptionally 200, species in a day. It would be difficult to see more than seventy-five in one day in the Bahamas (sixty in an afternoon is my record), but it certainly is not true to say that 'there are almost no birds'. Yet this view is commonly held, and arises, I think, from the fact that there are few large birds likely to be seen soaring, few essentially aerial birds, few that are found in large numbers together, and few that are cheeky enough to attract the attention of unobservant people.

Hurricanes and their Effects

The popular explanation of this supposed lack of birds is that they have been destroyed by hurricanes. But the last hurricane to do serious damage on New Providence was in 1929, and one would expect the bird population to be back to normal within five or ten years. It is known that the Bahamas Government imported birds from Jamaica to restock New Providence, yet the advice on which it acted must be considered suspect, for one of the species imported, the White-bellied Dove, is the wildest and most retiring bird imaginable: one could loose ten thousand of them and never notice the difference. And one learns that after the last hurricane a hush fell over New Providence because there were no more songbirds, but this could be partly accounted for by the normal autumn cessation of song. I do not underestimate the power of a hurricane for I was in Florida during 'Donna' in 1960; what I question is the assumption that the destruction wrought in 1929 is still a factor in considering the bird population to-day.

Bird-tables

Many people in the Bahamas would like to attract more birds to their garden, and wonder how to do so. Gardens that start with an advantage are those that have well-grown trees, or trees bearing berries or fruit, and are adjacent to unspoiled country and not too close to the sea, but in almost any garden a bird-table will provide an added attraction. Our table, which though poorly attended in summer was a great success in winter, attracted the following species:

For fruit (oranges, sapodilla, raisins). Bananaquits, Catbirds, Cape May Warblers, Northern and Bahama Mockingbirds, Red-legged Thrushes, Yellow-bellied Sapsuckers.

For seed. Ground Doves, Indigo and Painted Buntings.

For bread. Palm Warblers, Ovenbirds, Yellowthroats.

Water is of course essential in addition to food, and the table should stand near a bush or other cover.

The chief problem that our bird-table presented, apart from rats and mice (solution: a rifle) and ants (solution: insecticide), was to prevent the Ground Doves from eating all the seed and chasing the other birds away. This we resolved by putting the seed in boxes attached to the underside of the main platform, where grassquits and buntings could cling to the boxes but a dove would bang its head on the platform above! The doves fought one another for their ration in a bowl on the ground.

Classification of Birds

Some 222 different species of birds are known from New Providence. They fall into the following broad categories:

Residents	40
Summer visitors	9
Winter visitors	70
Passage migrants	71
Vagrants and unclassified	32

These figures are only approximate, and are likely to change slightly in the course of time. More than thirty species have been added to the list for New Providence in the past few years, and the same is true of the Bahamas as a whole. The end of this adding-to-the-list process is not yet in sight, for it seems that almost any species of migratory bird that reaches south Florida will occasionally overreach itself and turn up in the Bahamas, particularly in the northern islands.

SOURCES

New Providence

This book is based on my own observations during nearly four and a half years' residence on New Providence, from December 1958 to April 1963. I have supplemented them with information obtained from the late Robert S. Hanlon Jr and Brother Ignatius Deàn, who very kindly allowed me to use their records, which are mostly from the vicinity of St Augustine's Monastery, Nassau. Records from this source are marked *. Any records for New Providence obtained from other sources are marked †.

Out Islands

For information on the out islands I have drawn on all the relevant material that I have been able to obtain. Most of this is summarised by James Bond, together with other information collected by him, in his *Check-list of the Birds of the West Indies* and supplements, but where possible I have gone back to the original sources. Records obtained by Mr C. Russell Mason in Grand Bahama and elsewhere have been particularly valuable. I have also drawn on my own records for the out islands, but these cover from a few days to a few weeks on four islands only.

NOTES ON SUB-HEADINGS

To clarify any ambiguous points, I append a list of notes on the sub-headings used in the text:

Names These follow the A.O.U. Check-list of North American Birds for all species there listed, and Bond's *Birds of the West Indies* for the others. I have been able to incorporate at the last moment most, if not all, of the changes which are to appear in the sixth edition of the A.O.U. Check-List.

Status, NP

NP signifies New Providence Island.

RESIDENT A breeding species, present all year round.

SUMMER VISITOR Arrives in the spring, breeds here, and leaves in the autumn.

WINTER VISITOR Passes the winter (and often a large part of the year) here, but does not breed.

PASSAGE MIGRANT Passes through in a northerly direction in spring and in a southerly direction in autumn. Neither breeds nor passes the winter here.

VAGRANT Occurs irregularly, with movements that do not conform to any apparent pattern.

Not recorded Not recorded, but may occur occasionally.

Not found Not recorded, and not likely to be recorded.

The foregoing expressions are usually accompanied by an adjective indicating the commonness of each species. 'Abundant', 'common', 'fairly common', and 'uncommon' are not likely to be misunderstood, but 'rare' is used to imply 'of rare but regular occurrence', while 'occasional' implies 'of very rare and irregular occurrence'.

I have described in approximate terms (e.g. early April, mid-September) the times of arrival and departure of migrant birds. Unless otherwise stated these times are when the species is first found, or ceases to be found, *in substantial numbers*. The 'early and late dates' or 'extreme dates', on the other hand, are the extreme known limits of occurrence of a species, and habitually refer to unusually precocious individuals or to laggards that remain when the main body has left. There is therefore no anomaly in the statement 'arrives in mid-September. ... early date, 20 August'. The information on the commoner species is backed by countless observations, but the time of arrival and departure of rarer species is stated in vaguer terms (e.g. 'September'), and their extreme dates are shown in brackets, indicating that these records perhaps tell an incomplete story.

Status, Out Is Out Islands is a term meaning all the Bahama Islands except New Providence. cf. **Status, NP.**

It should be noted with regard to out-island distribution that a lot of useful field-work has been done on some islands, mostly in the north, and almost none on others. A study of the resulting records and dates tells one almost more about people than about birds: one records Mr Mason on Grand Bahama, Mr Collett on Eleuthera, and so on, and notes a dearth of observers on certain other islands, such as Long Is and Crooked Is; but a clear picture of the *bird* distribution is harder to reach. To avoid recording a 'spotty' and probably false distribution for many species, I have added the *probable* distribution to the *known* distribution, as in 'recorded only from Gd. Bahama and San Salvador, but probably occurs on all islands on migration'.

I have shown dates of occurrence of migrant birds, when known to me, only when they fall outside the early and late dates given for New Providence. I have confined this work to the Bahamas as a political entity, although to be complete geographically the archipelago would include the Turks and Caicos Islands and would exclude Cay Sal and Cay Lobos.

Description, habits This section is prefaced by the approximate length of each species in inches. In about two-thirds of the species there is little difference between the plumage of males and females, and in such cases the notation 's A' (=sexes alike) appears after the length.

Voice I have treated the commoner resident species at some length in the belief that some of this information may not have been published before. A song chart of certain species will be found on page 132.

ILLUSTRATIONS

The illustrations—four coloured plates and nine black-and-white ones—have been done by Hermann Heinzel. All the important resident land birds of the Bahamas have been illustrated in colour, some for the first time.

Our criterion in deciding which species to illustrate has been to show, first, all the resident and regular Bahaman breeding species and, second, all species not illustrated by Roger Tory Peterson in his *Field Guide to the Birds*. This book will thus serve as a complement to Peterson's Guide (or to other North American Guides) in covering this area, and to facilitate its use in this way Peterson's plate numbers are shown in the text, with the notation 'RTP' before them. Our own plate numbers are shown, in darker type, as 'Pl . . .'

ACKNOWLEDGEMENTS

I would like to record my gratitude to:

Robert S. Arbib, Jr, of Mamoroneck, New York
Brother Ignatius Dean, of St Augustine's Monastery, Nassau
The late Robert W. Hanlon, Jr, of St Augustine's Monastery, Nassau
Mrs Margaret Hundley, of Maitland, Florida
C. Russell Mason, of Maitland, Florida
Dennis R. Paulson, of Miami, Florida
William B. Robertson, Jr, of Homestead, Florida
Oris S. Russell, of Nassau
Alexander Sprunt IV, of Tavernier, Florida

for their encouragement, advice, or for use of their records. My indebtedness to Brother Ignatius Dean, in particular, is immeasurable.

GREBES
Podicipedidae

LEAST GREBE *Podiceps dominicus* (Formerly Mexican Grebe)   Pl 2
Status: NP: UNCOMMON RESIDENT. Out Is: recorded from most main islands except Gd. Bahama and Abaco.
Description, habits: L 9″ S A. Least Grebes are distinguished from the next species by their *small size, thin, dark bills,* and mainly *white wings* (noticeable only in flight). Plumage: mostly smoke-grey with a blackish cap. Eyes: orange. There is no great difference between this and the next species in general appearance and habits: both are round, almost tailless diving birds, rarely seen out of the water. The Least Grebe is by far the less common of the two, frequenting only two or three ponds on New Providence (and one on Paradise Is), where they are usually found in pairs or family parties, keeping close to the edge and disappearing among reeds and other vegetation when alarmed.
Voice: generally silent except in the breeding season, when a trilling 'werrererererererr' or 'kwelelelelelek' is heard. A loud 'ek' seems to denote mild alarm, and a sharp 'steep' or 'eek', acute anxiety.
Nest: a small, floating platform of reeds or other plants. Both this and the next species cover the eggs with loose vegetation before leaving the nest, so that it appears to be a formless, rotting mass. The few nests that I have seen (May to September) contained 2 to 4 white eggs.

PIED-BILLED GREBE *Podilymbus podiceps*   Pl 2; RTP 1
Status: NP: COMMON RESIDENT. Out Is: to be expected throughout the Bahamas, though not recorded from all islands.
Description, habits: L 13″ S A. This is by far *the commoner of the two grebes,* and is noticeably *larger* than the last species. It has a large, rounded, *pale bill,* crossed by a vertical black line in summer. Plumage: brownish, with white under tail-coverts. Pied-billed Grebes are common on many lakes and ponds on New Providence. On Lake Cunningham they are common in winter yet relatively scarce in summer; this may indicate the presence of winter visitors from the north, or may simply represent a seasonal change of habitat, smaller stretches of water probably being more satisfactory for nesting.
Voice: a series of 'cow-cow-cow-cow-cow-cow-cowk' notes in summer.
Nest: a heap of weeds, sometimes floating, sometimes on mud, hard to distinguish from any other pile of damp vegetation. About 3 to 5 whitish eggs are laid; the nesting season extends from April to mid-October.

SHEARWATERS and PETRELS
Procellariidae

AUDUBON'S SHEARWATER *Puffinus lherminieri* (Local name: Pimlico)
Pls 1, 7; RTP 4

Status: NP: not likely to be seen from land, but found in nearby waters. Out Is: recorded at sea throughout the Bahamas.

Description: L 11½″ s A. This, the common shearwater of the Bahamas, has blackish upperparts, white underparts, and a short, rounded tail. It is known by its long, narrow wings and its habit of flying and gliding low over the sea, often disappearing into the troughs of waves. Common, and apparently resident in Bahamian waters. Breeds on suitable cays but, as it only comes to land at night, and nests in burrows and cavities, there are few positive nesting records. One white egg is laid, in early spring.

STORM PETRELS
Hydrobatidae

WILSON'S PETREL, *Oceanites oceanicus,* and **LEACH'S PETREL,** *Oceanodroma leucorhoa.* **RTP 4**

Petrels are *oceanic birds*, most likely to be seen flying effortlessly, far from land. They are known by their *small size* (7″ to 9″), dark plumage, and white rumps. Wilson's is distinguished by its square tail, long legs (the feet protrude beyond the tail), and skimming flight; Leach's by its paler plumage, forked tail, and erratic flight. Wilson's often follows ships; Leach's rarely does. Both species are known to occur in Bahamian waters on passage or in summer. Wilson's has the distinction of nesting in the Antarctic and migrating north for its winter (our summer)—a reversal of the normal state of affairs—and appears to be the commoner species. When feeding, it flutters over the sea with dangling feet, 'walking' on the water.

TROPICBIRDS
Phaëthontidae

WHITE-TAILED TROPICBIRD *Phaëthon lepturus* (Formerly Yellow-billed Tropicbird) **Pl 1**

Status: NP: not found. Out Is: a summer visitor, nesting in small colonies on suitable islands and cays.

Description: L 32″ (tail 16″) s A. A white, pigeon-like bird of the open sea, known by the two long tail-feathers that stream out behind it. The white plumage is marked with black on the wings and back. Immatures lack the long tail-feathers, and have the upperparts heavily speckled with black. Adults have red bills, immatures yellow.

PELICANS
Pelecanidae

BROWN PELICAN *Pelecanus occidentalis*   RTP 8
Status: NP: Occasionally recorded—eg. 31 October†. Evidently a RARE VAGRANT. Out Is: occurs infrequently from Andros and Eleuthera north-wards, and commonly at Inagua, but apparently not between. Different sub-species are involved, one straying southward from Florida and the other northward from the Antilles. Formerly bred in the Biminis.
Description: L 50″ s A. The odd shape of this ungainly seabird is known to most people since their childhood. The plumage is dark-brown except for a variable area of white on the head and neck. When standing, the large bill carried flat against the neck is distinctive. It flies with alternating spells of flapping and gliding, and makes sudden plunges into the sea.

BOOBIES
Sulidae

BLUE-FACED BOOBY *Sula dactylatra*   Pl 1; RTP 3
Status: NP: not found. Out Is: a small colony used to nest, and probably still does, on Santo Domingo Cay, south of the Ragged Is.
Description: L 32″ s A. Boobies are fast-flying seabirds, distinguished from gulls and terns by their large size, powerful beaks, and pointed tails. The Blue-faced is a *mainly white* booby with a black tail and black on the tips and rear edges of the wings. Far less common than the following species.

BROWN BOOBY *Sula leucogaster* (Formerly White-bellied Booby)
                                                        Pl 1; RTP 3
Status: NP: not found. Out Is: nests early in the spring on small cays and rocks, notably in the southern Bahamas. At other times of year should be looked for well out to sea.
Description: L 29″ s A. The plumage is *mainly dark-brown*, with an exten-sive area of white on the undersides of the wings and on the underparts. The sharp division between the dark head and neck and the white breast is particularly noticeable.

Plate 1

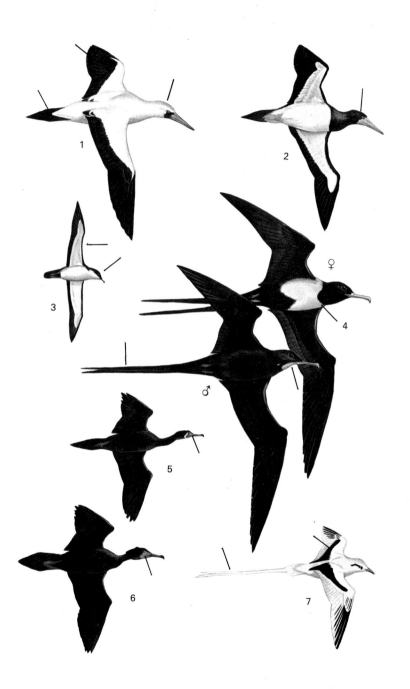

1 summary
winter

2 summer
winter

3

4

5 ♀
♂

6

7

Plate 2

CORMORANTS
Phalacrocoracidae

DOUBLE-CRESTED CORMORANT *Phalacrocorax auritus* **Pl 1; RTP 3**
Status: NP: RARE VAGRANT. Only 3 records: 3 and 25* April, 26 June.
Out Is: resident in the northern Bahamas, south to Andros and Eleuthera,
and found irregularly farther south.
Description, habits: L 32″ S A. A large and, in adult plumage, *all-black*
seabird, with a *long, snaky head and neck*; immatures have whitish underparts. Cormorants frequent lakes or sea coast, and swim with backs awash
and long bills pointed up at an angle, or sit upright on rocks or posts,
often holding their wings open to dry. They are one of the many seabirds
which, though found on nearby islands, are usually absent from New
Providence.

OLIVACEOUS CORMORANT *Phalacrocorax olivaceus* (Formerly
Mexican Cormorant) **Pl 1**
Status: NP: not found. Out Is: breeds on San Salvador and Inagua, and is
to be expected on the intervening islands.
Description: L 26″ S A. Similar to the preceding species, but *smaller*, with a
white border to the throat in the breeding season.

FRIGATEBIRDS
Fregatidae

MAGNIFICENT FRIGATEBIRD *Fregata magnificens* (Other name:
Man-o'-War Bird) **Pl 1; RTP 13**
Status: NP: RARE VAGRANT. Recorded in March, May, September, and
December, and no doubt occurs at other times. Out Is: Resident. Present
round the coasts of most islands, nesting on small cays.
Description, habits: L 40″ (wingspan 7½ ft.). Suggestive of its name, this is
a magnificent, *long-winged seabird, usually seen soaring* effortlessly high
over the sea. Adult males have entirely black plumage; adult females are
similar but show a white breast-patch, while immatures have the whole
head and underparts white. Adult males have a curious, inflatable throat-
pouch, bright red in the breeding season, but not visible at a distance.
Although widely distributed in the Bahamas, frigatebirds are seldom seen
from New Providence. The island's unsuitability as a nesting site is an
b vious reason, and the lack of fish-eating seabirds to rob may be another.

HERONS and BITTERNS
Ardeidae

GREAT BLUE HERON *Ardea herodias* (Local name: Arsnicker) RTP 20
Status: NP: FAIRLY COMMON WINTER VISITOR. Arrives in late October
and in November, and leaves again by May, but stragglers remain till late
summer and possibly all through the year, the only month in which I have
not seen them being August. Extreme dates: 24 Sept, 26 July. Out Is:
occurs throughout the Bahamas in winter.
Description, habits: L 48″ S A. The Great Blue Heron is the largest bird
found on New Providence. Its *great size*, *long legs*, and *long neck* (folded
in flight), are usually sufficient to identify it. Plumage: blue-grey with
mostly white headfeathers; bill, yellow. Except when on migration or
newly arrived, the Great Blue is a solitary bird, most often seen by pond,
swamp, or mudflat, stalking about in shallow water or standing motionless
on the edge.

GREEN HERON *Butorides virescens* (Local name: Poor Joe) Pl 3; RTP 21
Status: NP: COMMON RESIDENT. Out Is: common resident on all islands.
Description, habits: L 18″ S A. *A small, dark, and noisy heron*, the commonest
of its family on New Providence. The plumage is variable: in full breeding
plumage it has a black cap, chestnut neck, grey body with shiny blue-green
feathers on the back, and bright orange legs. At other seasons the legs
are greenish and the plumage brown, streaked with white on the underparts. Like all herons, it has a long neck and a strong, spear-shaped bill.
 The Green Heron is *best identified by its habits*, for it is tame yet hys-
terical, bold yet skulking. When alarmed it slinks about in a crouching
posture, betraying its nervousness by flicking its tail and raising and lower-
ing its shaggy crest, making, it always seems to me, rather pathetic attempts
at concealment. Or, when surprised by the edge of some muddy pool, it
flies up with loud, agonised calls, audible a mile away. But it freely visits
gardens, where it feeds on lizards, and I have seen it within a yard or two
of my windows. Any piece of water down to the merest puddle attracts this
heron, but it will feed, roost, and nest at a distance from water. Unlike
other herons, it neither roosts nor nests in colonies, and so is found evenly
distributed in suitable places all through the year. Habitat: mangrove
swamps, ponds, rocky sea coast, swampy or flooded land, gardens and
woodland.
Voice: various squawking and chacking sounds are made. When alarmed,

gives a long series of raucous calls: 'kaaa, kaaa, kaaa, kew, kew, kew, kaaa, kaaa, kuk kuk kuk', etc.

Nest: a smallish, loosely made cup of sticks, placed from low to medium height in a tree or bush, for preference a mangrove. Most nests are difficult to approach as the mangrove swamps are usually impassable during the rainy summer season. The nests I have seen contained two or three young; three is stated to be the usual clutch in the West Indies. The eggs are described as pale bluish-green. The breeding season extends from April to about September.

LITTLE BLUE HERON *Florida caerulea*   Pl 3; RTP 20

Status: NP: COMMON WINTER VISITOR, arriving from August onwards and leaving again in April and May. A number of non-breeding individuals, in intermediate plumage (see below), are found in June and July, so the species is present all year round. Out Is: common throughout the Bahamas, nesting on many islands.

Description, habits: L 25″ s A. Adults have a *uniform dark-blue plumage*, with a purplish tinge on the head and neck in the breeding season. Immatures, which are twice as numerous as adults and much more noticeable, have *pure white plumage*, and are distinguished from egrets by their *blue bills*, tipped with black, and *greenish legs* and feet. When the immature white feathers are being replaced by the dark adult ones, a weird, irregular mixture of blue and white results. This is seen from March to July, though a few white feathers may remain until October or November. The Little Blue is, with the exception of the familiar Green Heron, the commonest of its family on New Providence. It is found in ones or twos, alone or with other herons or egrets, frequenting ponds, swamps, flooded land, and mudflats. This heron is often shot by irresponsible people; it is, or was, killed for food on some islands, but this is not the case on New Providence, where its destruction is not only illegal but pointless.

CATTLE EGRET *Bubulcus ibis* (Former English name: Buff-backed Heron)   Pl 3

Status: NP: FAIRLY COMMON WINTER VISITOR. A few, presumably non-breeding, birds are found in summer, so the species is present all year round. Out Is: no doubt occurs on all main islands. Common on Eleuthera in winter.

Description, habits: L 20″ s A. A relatively small, *white* heron with a *yellow bill* and dark legs. The similarly coloured Great Egret is twice as large and almost invariably found by water. From March until August most Cattle Egrets are in breeding plumage, with rich buff plumes on the head, breast, and back, and yellowish or reddish legs. Cattle Egrets *habitually feed among cattle* or horses. On New Providence there are few cattle, so they are more likely to be seen on golf courses, particularly at Lyford Cay. They are usually *not found by water*, except when roosting in mangroves. They are commonest in spring and autumn, which suggests a passage movement between, perhaps, wintering grounds on Eleuthera and breeding colonies on Andros. Although gregarious, single birds are often seen on New Providence, but two, three, four, or up to ten birds together are more usual, and I have seen as many as thirty together on migration.

REDDISH EGRET *Dichromanassa rufescens*   **Pl 3; RTP 20**
Status: NP: RARE VAGRANT. July (31st) to November (21st). Out Is: apparently fairly common on Andros and Gt. Inagua, nesting (and resident ?) on both islands. Seldom recorded, but probably occurs irregularly, on the other islands.
Description, habits: L 30″ s A. Reddish Egrets are found in two colour phases—dark and white—unrelated to the age or sex of the birds. In the dark phase, adults have reddish-brown head and neck feathers and the rest of the plumage grey, while in the white phase the plumage is uniformly white. In either plumage the *bill is flesh-coloured* with a black tip, the legs bluish, and the neck feathers noticeably shaggy. Immatures have dark, blackish bills and legs and, in the dark phase, lack most of the red-brown feathers, and are rather hard to identify except by a process of elimination.
Reddish Egrets are usually found by the sea, particularly on mudflats, where they rush about after fish in a most undignified and un-heronlike way. In 1960 a party of four immatures (3 white, 1 dark) remained nearly four months in the South Beach region; they had probably wandered there from Andros. I have only recorded this species once since then.

GREAT EGRET *Casmerodius albus*
(Formerly Common or American Egret)   **Pl 3; RTP 20**
Status: NP: UNCOMMON WINTER VISITOR. Like other herons that nest on nearby islands, this species occurs nearly all year round: July (23rd) to June (3rd). Out Is: found throughout the Bahamas, nesting on some islands.
Description, habits: L 39″ s A. This is *the largest of the white-plumaged herons* found on New Providence. The plumage is pure white, the *bill*

yellow, the legs and feet black. It is a relatively scarce bird, usually found in only two or three places on the island: there is, for instance, a party of five that spends the winter fishing in the sea at the mouth of Miller Sound, and there is, or was, an individual that fished the Lyford Cay ponds each year. Away from such chosen spots it occurs only irregularly.

SNOWY EGRET *Leucophoyx thula* RTP 20

Status: NP: FAIRLY COMMON WINTER VISITOR. Normally arrives in October and leaves in April and May, though an occasional individual is seen in the intervening months. Extreme dates: 19 August, 28 May. Also, exceptionally, 3 July. Out Is: presumably occurs throughout the Bahamas, though not recorded from all islands. Stated, surprisingly, to be rare.

Description, habits: L 24″ S A. A medium-sized, *pure white* heron, distinguished by its mainly black bill and legs, and *yellow feet*. The Snowy Egret is the commonest white heron after the immature Little Blue. While best identified by the different colour of the bill, legs, and feet, the egret is noticeably more graceful, and can with practice be distinguished from the heavier-built Little Blue by its shape alone. It frequents mangrove swamps, pools, and flooded land, alone or with other herons and egrets.

LOUISIANA HERON *Hydranassa tricolor* (Other name: Tricolored Heron) Pl 3; RTP 20

Status: NP: FAIRLY COMMON RESIDENT. Out Is: found throughout the Bahamas. Often common.

Description, habits: L 26″ S A. This is the only *dark-plumaged heron with white underparts*, the upperparts and long neck being blue-grey, the belly white. Immature birds have chestnut-coloured necks, which makes them 'tricolored'. The Louisiana Heron appears to be the only large heron that nests on New Providence but, even so, it is not particularly common. Outside the breeding season it is found singly or in groups, sometimes with Little Blue Herons or Snowy Egrets. It shows a greater fondness for mangrove swamps (or perhaps a greater fear of human beings) than most other herons.

Nest: of sticks, placed on mangroves. 3 or 4 bluish-green eggs are laid, probably mostly in May. I know of only one small nesting colony on New Providence, in an inaccessible mangrove on the southern part of the island, but there may be others.

BLACK-CROWNED NIGHT HERON *Nycticorax nycticorax* (English name: Night Heron)   RTP 21

Status: NP: RARE VAGRANT. Only two certain records (adults): 18 March and 1 June. Out Is: recorded from the northern Bahamas and from Inagua, no doubt occurring in between.

Description, habits: L 25″ s A. Adults are identified by their stocky build, *black back* and crown, *grey wings* and tail, and whitish face and underparts. Immatures are brown-plumaged and are easily confused with immature Yellow-crowned Night Herons, or even with American Bitterns. Bitterns show a dark mark on the neck, and have black wingtips which are distinctive in flight; while Yellow-crowned Night Herons have longer legs which, in flight, extend well beyond the tail. The Black-crowned is surprisingly rare on New Providence, though possibly not as rare as my two records suggest, as I have some records of immatures that might refer to either species of night heron. The Black-crowned is a more nocturnal bird than the next, and this no doubt contributes to its apparent rarity.

YELLOW-CROWNED NIGHT HERON *Nyctanassa violacea*
                                                                                  Pl 3; RTP 21

Status: NP: presumed a WINTER VISITOR. Uncommon. Noted during every month of the year except June and August. One isolated July (24th) record. Out Is: found throughout the Bahamas, nesting on many islands. Formerly abundant and probably still common in places.

Description, habits: L 25″ s A. Adult plumage is uniformly *pale-grey* except for the head, which is black with a white crown and *cheek-mark*. The legs are yellow, the bill dark. Immatures have brown plumage and can be confused with immature Black-crowned Night Herons or with American Bitterns. The latter are known in flight by their blackish wingtips, the former by their short legs which, in flight, barely extend beyond the tail.

   Yellow-crowned Night Herons feed principally on crabs, but will take frogs and other suitable food, in search of which they stray from their usual swampy habitat into fields and even on to roads (twice noted). They are not strictly nocturnal, but sufficiently so to make it difficult to estimate their numbers and status: from time to time one comes on an individual resting by day in thick mangroves and many others may—or may not—be doing the same. I do not believe that they nest on New Providence, but it is hard to be sure.

Plate 3

1. **Green Heron** page 23
   Small, dark, noisy, common.
   Adult: chestnut neck; orange legs.
   Immature: brownish, streaked.

2. **Yellow-crowned Night Heron** 27
   Adult: grey plumage; black-and-white head pattern.
   Immature: brown; speckled back. See text.

3. **Least Bittern** 30
   Very small. Secretive. Buff wing-patches.

4. **Little Blue Heron** 24
   Adult: uniform dark-blue plumage; blue bill.
   Immature: uniform white plumage; blue bill.
   1 yr.: irregular blue and white plumage.

5. **Louisiana Heron** 26
   Dark plumage; white belly.

6. **Cattle Egret** 24
   Breeding: mainly white plumage; buff plumes on head,
     back and breast.
   Non-breeding: uniform white plumage; yellow bill,
     black legs.
   Small size. Fields.

7. **Great Egret** 25
   Uniform white plumage; yellow bill, black legs. Large
     size. By water.

8. **Reddish Egret** 25
   White phase: uniform white plumage. Usually flesh-coloured
     bill.
   Dark phase: dark plumage. Usually flesh-coloured bill.
   Salt water. See text.

1
immature
adult

2
ad.
immature

3
♀
♂

4
1year
immature
adult

5
ad.

6
non breeding

7

8
white phase
dark phase

1

2

3

4

♂

♀

Plate 4

1. **Turkey Vulture** page 37
   Perched: large, dark. Red head (adults).
   Flying: large, dark; wings paler. Usually soaring.

2. **Red-tailed Hawk** 38
   Perched: brown plumage; rufous tail.
   Flying: round-winged; rufous tail.

3. **Osprey** 39
   Perched: dark upperparts; white head and underparts.
   Flying: narrow wings with black patches; white underparts.

4. **American Kestrel** 40
   Perched: small size; face pattern; rufous back and tail.
   Flying: pointed wings; black-tipped, rufous tail.

LEAST BITTERN *Ixobrychus exilis*   Pl 3; RTP 21
Status: NP: FAIRLY COMMON RESIDENT. Out Is: only recorded from
Andros, Gd. Bahama, Eleuthera, and San Salvador, but is to be expected
on other islands.
Description, habits: L 12½″ This is *the smallest of the herons*. Male plumage
is distinctive: black on the crown and back, and different tones of buff
and chestnut on the wings and underparts. Females are browner and more
nondescript, but both sexes show large *buff wing-patches* in flight. Green
Herons have dark wings. Least Bitterns are secretive birds and hard to
observe. They are most often seen as they suddenly take flight from among
thick, aquatic vegetation, fly a short distance, and drop out of sight again.
They frequent mangrove swamps and their vicinity and are most in evidence in the spring and summer months.
Nest: stated to make a small nest low down in aquatic vegetation, laying
up to 5 bluish- or greenish-white eggs.

AMERICAN BITTERN *Botaurus lentiginosus*   RTP 21
Status: NP: UNCOMMON WINTER VISITOR. Arrives later and leaves earlier
than most winter visitors. October (23rd) to March (3rd). Also, exceptionally, 23 April. Out Is: very little data; presumably occurs sparingly
throughout the Bahamas in winter.
Description, habits: L 30″ S A. *A heavily-built, brown heron*, most often
seen when unexpectedly flushed; it then rises with croaks of alarm and
flies off some distance before settling again. The *blackish wingtips* are the
best field mark in flight and distinguish the bittern from the otherwise
similar immature night herons. On the ground the brown plumage, black
stripe on the neck, streaked underparts, and greenish legs, make it difficult
to see, especially in thick cover. American Bitterns inhabit mangrove
swamps, reed-fringed ponds, flooded land, and fields of thick grass, and
appear to remain in the same place all winter as I have sometimes flushed
one from the same spot week after week.

IBISES and SPOONBILLS
Threskiornithidae

GLOSSY IBIS *Plegadis falcinellus*   RTP 21
Status: NP: UNCOMMON PASSAGE MIGRANT and vagrant. February (2nd)
to May (27th); August (30th) to October (27th). Also 19–21 June and 7
July. Out Is: recorded from a number of islands (including 9, Exuma,

1 April (B–B)) and no doubt occurs throughout the Bahamas. Late date: Gd. Bahama, 26 November.

Description, habits: L 23″ s A. *A large, uniformly dark wading bird* with a long, *decurved bill*. In good light the dark, chestnut-coloured plumage will be seen to be beautifully glossed with bronze and green. Glossy Ibises are sociable birds by choice, but they occur here singly or in threes and fours. A small group often stays by a pond for several weeks before moving on; the birds feed voraciously with the whole head submerged, and take little notice of cars or human beings. Formerly described as rare vagrants, they are of regular occurrence on New Providence.

WHITE IBIS *Eudocimus albus*   RTP 21
Status: NP: only one record, 22 October, an immature. Presumably an OCCASIONAL VAGRANT. Out Is: recorded from Andros (Oct), Gd. Bahama (Oct, Nov), and Gt. Inagua (July). No doubt occurs on other islands at times.
Description: L 25″ s A. Adults are unmistakable: the whole plumage, except for the black wingtips, is *white*; the face and *long, curved bill* are red. Immatures have brown upperparts, brownish heads and necks, white rumps and underparts, and pinkish bills. White Ibises that occur in the northern Bahamas are likely to be wanderers from Florida, where the species is relatively common.

ROSEATE SPOONBILL *Ajaia ajaja*   Pl 2; RTP 20
Status: NP: not found. Out Is: nests in small numbers on Gt. Inagua. Rare vagrant elsewhere.
Description: L 32″ s A. The spoonbill is a *mainly pink* wading bird with a scarlet patch on the shoulders, a bare, featherless head, and a large, *spoon-shaped bill*. It is a shorter, stouter bird than the flamingo, and has no black wing-feathers.

FLAMINGOS
Phoenicopteridae

AMERICAN FLAMINGO *Phoenicopterus ruber*   Pl 2; RTP 20
Status: NP: no recent records, but is a possible vagrant. Can be seen, of course, in captivity. Out Is: an important breeding colony is situated on

Gt. Inagua, and smaller colonies may still exist on Andros and Abaco.
Vagrant elsewhere.

Description: L 45″ s A. The *long legs and neck* and *pink plumage* identify
the celebrated flamingo; in flight large black areas on the wings become
visible. This species is so much talked and written about, usually with
reference to the Bahamas, that many people mistakenly expect to see it on
New Providence.

GEESE and DUCKS
Anatidae

SNOW GOOSE *Chen hyperborea*   RTP 10, 11
Status: NP: no recent records, but to be looked for in winter. Out Is:
scattered records from Gd. Bahama (most recent record, 12 November)
to Inagua. Evidently an occasional winter visitor.
Description: L about 28″ s A. Snow Geese occur in two colour phases,
white and blue (the latter until recently considered a distinct species, the
Blue Goose), but will be known from ducks and other water birds by
their large size and longish necks. Their plumages are:
a   all white*, with black wingtips (adult white phase)
b   pale, greyish (immature white phase)
c   grey, with white* head, upper neck, and tail-coverts (adult blue phase)
d   brownish, with pale tail-coverts (imm. blue phase).
* The white feathers are often stained with rust.
Adults are stated to be rarer than immatures.

WEST INDIAN TREE DUCK *Dendrocygna arborea*   Pl 2
Status: NP: no recent records. Out Is: recorded only from Andros, San
Salvador, and Inagua. Apparently still breeds on Inagua.
Description: L 20″ s A. A long-legged, goose-shaped duck of nocturnal
habits. Perches in trees. Plumage mostly brown, paler and speckled on
the underparts.

MALLARD *Anas platyrhynchos*   RTP 15, 18, 19
Status: NP: no recent records; formerly occurred in winter. Out Is: recorded from Andros in winter; and, recently Gd. Bahama (23 November
and late December) and Eleuthera (4 December); evidently an occasional
winter visitor to the northern Bahamas.
Description: L 23″ The progenitor of the common farmyard duck. Males
are known by their *green heads*, white-ringed necks and rufous chests.

The female is a plain, brown duck, similar to a female Pintail but distinguished by its white-bordered, blue speculum and its partly orange-coloured bill.

PINTAIL *Anas acuta*   RTP 15, 18, 19
Status: NP: RARE PASSAGE MIGRANT. March (25th); September (29th) to October (13th). Out Is: only recorded from Gd. Bahama (late autumn date, 24 November) and Abaco, but no doubt occurs sparingly on all islands.
Description: L 25″ Male plumage is mainly grey, with a *brown head*, white neck with a thin white line running on to the head, and a *long, pointed tail*. The female is a plain, brown, grey-billed duck with a slender neck and pointed tail. Pintail are rare visitors to New Providence, only occurring singly and on migration. They seek the company of whatever other ducks they can find, usually Blue-winged Teal.

BAHAMA DUCK *Anas bahamensis* (Formerly Bahama Pintail; other name: White-cheeked Pintail)   Pl 2
Status: NP: only seen one year: April (28th) to May (13th). Evidently an OCCASIONAL PASSAGE MIGRANT. Out Is: known to be fairly common on certain islands (eg. Abaco, Gt. Inagua), and recorded from many other islands. Presumably occurs throughout the Bahamas, though to what extent it is a summer visitor (local name: summer duck) is uncertain.
Description: L 17″ S A. A brown-bodied duck with conspicuous *white cheeks and throat* and a mainly *red bill*. The pointed tail is light-buff, the speculum green. Bahama Ducks are very rare on New Providence, perhaps only occurring on their way to and from their nesting grounds on Andros, Abaco, etc.

GREEN-WINGED TEAL *Anas carolinensis*   RTP 15, 18, 19
Status: NP: RARE PASSAGE MIGRANT, occasional winter visitor. March (18th–24th); October (12th) to November (22nd). Also 19 January. Out Is: seldom recorded, but no doubt occurs on most islands on migration. Late spring date: Gd. Bahama, 10 April.
Description: L 14″ The male in breeding plumage is identified by its chestnut head, with a broad, green band running back from the eye. Females, immatures, or moulting males are commoner on New Providence, and they are virtually indistinguishable on the water from female Blue-winged Teal (q.v.). However, the two species are easily distinguished in

flight, when the 'greenwing' shows a metallic *green stripe* along the *rear edge* of the wing, while the 'bluewing' (in addition to a similar green stripe) shows a large, pale-blue patch on the front edge of the wing. Green-winged Teal occur singly or in small parties, sometimes among 'bluewings', and usually in the autumn.

BLUE-WINGED TEAL *Anas discors*   RTP 15, 18, 19

Status: NP: FAIRLY COMMON WINTER VISITOR. Arrives mostly in September and October; leaves in April. Extreme dates: 21 July, 29 April. Out Is: no doubt found throughout the Bahamas in winter, though there are surprisingly few records.

Description, habits: L 15″ A small, mottled brown duck, identified in flight by the *pale-blue patches on the front half of the wings*; these may appear white from a distance. Males change into breeding plumage in December, and from then on show a distinctive white crescent on the face and another white patch near the tail, the rest of the body being pinkish-brown.

Blue-winged Teal are *the commonest ducks* on New Providence (except on Lake Cunningham, where scaup predominate). They are usually found in small groups of up to a dozen birds on pools among the mangroves, but are not easily noticed as they keep away from open water. They sometimes form rafts of 50 to 100 birds on Lake Cunningham, but this is unusual. Pairing takes place in March and April, some pairs being found separately, others associating with other pairs.

Voice: males utter distinctive peeping notes, which are often one's first indication of the presence of teal.

AMERICAN WIGEON *Mareca americana* (Other name: Baldpate)
RTP 15, 18, 19

Status: NP: UNCOMMON WINTER VISITOR. August (7th) to May (6th). Out Is: recorded from Andros, Eleuthera, Gd. Bahama and Acklins, no doubt occurring occasionally on all main islands.

Description, habits: L 20″ A relatively large duck. The male is identified by its *white crown* and, in flight, the large white patches on the forewings. Females, if alone, are difficult to identify; their plumage is reddish-brown with a greyish head and white belly. Wigeon are distinctly uncommon on New Providence, though most years a few are found for a week or two among the scaup on Lake Cunningham. I have a few records from other parts of the island, including one of 16 birds together on Corry Sound.

SHOVELER *Spatula clypeata*   RTP 15, 18, 19
Status: NP: recorded only twice: 22 October, and once 'in winter'†.
Presumed an OCCASIONAL PASSAGE MIGRANT. Out Is: seldom recorded,
but likely to occur on most islands occasionally. Early date: Gd. Bahama,
1 October.
Description: L 19″ Shovelers are known by their *disproportionately long,
broad bills*. Males in full plumage have black-and-white plumage, bottle-
green heads, and chestnut flanks. Females and moulting males are plain,
brownish ducks that swim with their foreparts low in the water, as if
weighed down by their bills. In flight they show a pale-blue patch on the
forewing—in this resembling the smaller Blue-winged Teal.

WOOD DUCK *Aix sponsa*   RTP 14, 18, 19
Status: NP: RARE PASSAGE MIGRANT. February (26th) to April (9th);
November (7th) to December (6th). Out Is: only recorded from Gd.
Bahama and Eleuthera (early autumn date: 14 September), but no doubt
occurs on other islands on passage.
Description: L 18½″ The male in full plumage has a beautifully variegated,
iridescent plumage; the flowing *crest* at the back of the head and the white
patterning of the face are noticeable even if colours cannot be distinguished.
The female is a dull, brown-plumaged duck with a smaller, but still
noticeable, crest and a *white patch round the eye*. Wood Ducks occur rather
irregularly, and usually in ones and twos. They keep inconspicuously to
the edges of ponds and lakes, and sometimes remain a week or two in the
same place if not disturbed.

RING-NECKED DUCK *Aythya collaris*   RTP 12, 16, 17
Status: NP: FAIRLY COMMON WINTER VISITOR on Lake Cunningham.
October (27th) to March (20th). Out Is: no doubt found occasionally on
most islands in winter, though there are few definite records.
Description, habits: L 17″ Essentially similar in plumage to the Lesser
Scaup, the male 'ring-neck' is distinguished by the *white ring* towards the
tip of its dark bill, by a crescent-shaped white mark at the front end of its
pale flanks, and by its black back (scaup having grey backs). The brown-
plumaged female also has a pale ring on the bill, and if well seen will show
a white eyering and a suffused whitish face-patch (as compared with the
bright white face-patches of female scaup).
   Ring-necked Ducks are found in twos, threes, and larger groups (once,
18 February, over 100) among the scaup and coot that enliven Lake

Cunningham in winter. They arrive earlier than most scaup and so sometimes outnumber them in early winter, but are easily overlooked later on when the following species is at full strength.

LESSER SCAUP *Aythya affinis*   RTP 12

Status: NP: COMMON WINTER VISITOR on Lake Cunningham. Most scaup arrive in the second half of December or the first half of January, and leave in late March or early April. Their dates of arrival and departure and the numbers in which they appear are variable, no doubt according to weather conditions farther north. Extreme dates: 6 November, 17 April. Also exceptionally (perhaps a wounded bird), 15 May. Out Is: no doubt occurs sparingly throughout the Bahamas in winter, though there are few definite records.

Description, habits: L 17″ The male has a black head and chest, a grey back, black tail, and whitish underparts and flanks. This gives a distinct pattern to birds on the water, *both 'ends' and the back appearing dark, the flanks white*. Females have plain brown plumage with a distinctive *white patch* at the base of the bill.

As many as 1,000 Lesser Scaup may be seen on Lake Cunningham some winters, 300 being a more usual number. They are usually in one or two large flocks mixed with coot and Ring-necked Ducks. No other species of duck is found in such large flocks on New Providence, but they would soon be exterminated if shooting were permitted on Lake Cunningham. Occasionally noted on Lake Killarney, Big Pond, etc.

RUDDY DUCK *Oxyura jamaicensis*   RTP 14, 16, 17

Status: NP: A RARE AND IRREGULAR VISITOR, perhaps now resident. See below. Out Is: recorded only from Eleuthera, San Salvador and Inagua. Evidently rare and probably of irregular occurrence, as on New Providence.

Description, habits: L 15½″ The male is easily recognised by its *rufous plumage*, black cap, *white cheeks*, and blue bill. (This plumage is lost in winter by N. American ruddies but not by the local race.) Females are brown-plumaged, distinguished by their whitish cheeks crossed by a single dark line. Ruddies often cock their tail up vertically, a distinctive habit shared only by the following species. They are rather tame.

A colony of a dozen or more Ruddy Ducks established themselves on a lake near Cable Beach in June or July 1962, and a brood of six tiny ducklings appeared on 30 August, and another (also of six) on 17 November. The colony was later heavily persecuted—the flightless young being shot on the water—and the survivors moved to Lake Cunningham, where they remained all winter and spring up to the time I left. This species is therefore resident, or potentially resident, in some years, but almost certainly absent in others, as I never saw it before 1962.

Reported, in 1966, as still present and breeding near Cable Beach, and also established on Paradise Is.

MASKED DUCK *Oxyura dominica*   Pl 2
Status: NP: RARE VAGRANT, perhaps a passage migrant. May (11th); August (7th) to September (8th), all in 1962. Out Is: not recorded.
Description: L 13″ Male plumage is *rich chestnut* streaked with black, with a mainly *black head* (which distinguishes it from the similar but white-cheeked male Ruddy Duck), and a blue bill. The female is brown, heavily barred, with a dark crown, and a buff face crossed by *two* dark lines. Both sexes show white wing-patches in flight. They cock their tails vertically. Secretive. The above are the first Bahamian records (six records, three localities) of this Antillean duck, but as it is found as near as Cuba and occurs in Florida more records can be expected from the Bahamas.

HOODED MERGANSER *Lophodytes cucullatus*   RTP 14, 18, 19
Status: NP: recorded once, 5 December*, and there is a second probable record. Evidently an OCCASIONAL WINTER VISITOR. Out Is: recorded from Gd. Bahama, 22–25 November, and probably from north Eleuthera in February. To be expected occasionally in winter on other islands in the northern Bahamas.
Description: L 17½″ The male is known by its erectile crest, white with a black border. It has a white chest with two black bars on either side, a dark back, and brown flanks. The female is a dark-plumaged duck (distinguished from the Red-breasted Merganser (see Appendix) by its dark head and neck), with a brownish crest. The thin, merganser bill is always distinctive.

AMERICAN VULTURES
Cathartidae

TURKEY VULTURE *Cathartes aura* (Local name: Crow)   Pl 4; RTP 35
Status: NP: RARE VAGRANT. One or more individuals were present for several months (29 January to 28 May) in 1961. Also seen, in other years,

in April*, July†, and August. Out Is: resident on Andros, Gd. Bahama, and Abaco. Common in many places.

Description: L 30″ (wingspread 6 ft) s A. This is a *huge*, blackish bird, *usually seen soaring*. Part of the wings, as seen from below, are paler than the rest—dark-grey against black. The naked skin of the head is red on adults, black on immatures. These are harmless, indeed beneficial birds as their food consists of carrion and offal of all sorts, and for this reason they tend to gather round settlements and roads. It seems likely that the birds that visit New Providence come from Andros; what is strange is that they do not come over more often, for I imagine that the coast of New Providence is visible to a vulture soaring high over Andros.

HAWKS
Accipitridae

SHARP-SHINNED HAWK *Accipiter striatus*   RTP 33, 37
Status: NP: has been recorded; probably an OCCASIONAL WINTER VISITOR. Out Is: there are old records from Acklins and Inagua, and a recent one from Bimini, all in February, March, or April.
Description: L 12″ This is the only *small* hawk with short, *rounded wings*. The similar-sized Merlin and Kestrel have pointed wings.

RED-TAILED HAWK *Buteo jamaicensis*   Pl 4; RTP 32, 34
Status: NP: recorded once, many years ago. Out Is: apparently an uncommon resident on Andros, Gd. Bahama, and Abaco. Also recorded (vagrant ?) from Eleuthera and Inagua.
Description: L 21″ A large, brown-plumaged, round-winged hawk, most often seen soaring. Adults are known by the *rufous* upperside of the tail, but this is lacking on immatures, for which the white breast and dark belly provide the best field-mark.

MARSH HAWK *Circus cyaneus* (English name: Hen Harrier) RTP 33, 34
Status: NP: UNCOMMON WINTER VISITOR. October (21st*) to March (29th*). Out Is: presumably occurs throughout the Bahamas in winter, though not recorded from all islands. Early date: Gd. Bahama, 15 August.
Description, habits: L 19″–23″ With the exception of the Osprey, this is the only large hawk- or eagle-like bird seen at all frequently on New Providence. The male is pale-grey, the female brown, and both have a distinctive *white rump*, the field-mark of this species. Marsh Hawks are typically

seen flying over ponds, lakes, and mangroves, but also hunt over dry, open country. They quarter the ground with slow, gliding flight, and pounce down on their prey.

OSPREYS
Pandionidae

OSPREY *Pandion haliaetus*   **Pl 4; RTP 36**
Status: NP: UNCOMMON VAGRANT. Recorded during most months of the year, though seldom in summer. More than half the records are for October, suggesting an autumn passage, and there appears to be a less marked passage in the spring, notably in March and April. Out Is: found throughout the Bahamas; resident on most islands.
Description, habits: L 23″ (wingspread about 5½ ft) s A. Ospreys are large birds of prey most likely to be seen flying, usually over water, and identified by their dark upperparts and *white head and underparts*. Ospreys feed on fish; they fly at some height, often hovering, and plunge into the water feet first. They are fine and interesting birds, but not well suited to such a crowded island as New Providence.
Voice: loud, cheeping whistles.

FALCONS
Falconidae

PEREGRINE *Falco peregrinus* (Other name: Duck Hawk)   RTP 33, 37
Status: NP: OCCASIONAL WINTER VISITOR. I have recorded it only once, 26 February, but there are earlier records. Out Is: no doubt occurs sparingly throughout the Bahamas, though not recorded from all islands.
Description: L 18″ s A. A *large, fast-flying* hawk. Its narrow, pointed wings set it apart from the other larger birds of prey (e.g. Marsh Hawk) and its size and swift flight from its smaller and commoner relatives (Merlin and Kestrel). If well seen, the black-and-white patterning of the head, grey back, and barred underparts are distinctive.

MERLIN *Falco columbarius* (Formerly Pigeon Hawk)   RTP 33, 37
Status: NP: FAIRLY COMMON PASSAGE MIGRANT, UNCOMMON WINTER VISITOR. Arrives in October, coinciding with the main passage of warblers and other small birds. Becomes rather scarce by the end of November (moving on with the migratory wave). Such individuals as remain all

winter seem to leave by the end of February, birds seen later apparently being on migration. Extreme dates: 22 September, 2 May. Out Is: presumably found throughout the Bahamas in winter, though not recorded from all islands.

Description, habits: L 12″ The male has grey and the female brown upperparts, and both have heavily streaked underparts. The best field-mark is the *tail*, which is *barred with black*, but these markings are often difficult to distinguish from a distance, when the *pointed wings* and *swift, purposeful flight* are the only noticeable characteristics.

This small hawk is the commonest bird of prey on New Providence. It is found in woodlands, on golf courses, mudflats, and even in Nassau, terrorising flocks of Palm Warblers and other small migrants, and pursuing birds as large as Mourning Doves.

AMERICAN KESTREL *Falco sparverius* (Formerly Sparrow Hawk)
Pl 4; RTP 33, 37

Status: NP: UNCOMMON WINTER VISITOR. September (1st*) to April (15th). There is an old June record. Out Is: recorded from most main islands. A resident subspecies is found on San Salvador and Gt. Inagua, and is to be expected on intervening islands and also Cat Is.

Description, habits: L 10½″ Known in flight by its small size and *reddish tail*, and when perched by the black-and-white patterning of the head. The plumage generally is brownish, paler and less heavily streaked on the underparts than the Merlin. This is the less common of the two small hawks that winter on New Providence, and it is rather smaller and less fierce than the preceding species. Frequents open country. Normally hovers when hunting, but seldom does this on New Providence.

PHEASANTS, PARTRIDGES and QUAILS
Phasianidae

BOBWHITE *Colinus virginianus* (Local name: Quail)   **Pl 5; RTP 31**
Status: NP: COMMON RESIDENT. Out Is: not found.
Description, habits: L 9½″ *Rotund, short-legged, terrestrial birds* with speckled, reddish-brown plumage. Males have conspicuous white-patterned heads. Bobwhites are found in small coveys, of from 6 or 8 up to about 15 birds, breaking into separate pairs in April and coming together again when the young are well grown, in about September. They run very fast and only take flight in emergency, when they fly off in all directions with *fast, whirring flight*. This is an introduced species on New Providence

('introduced many years ago', Cory (1880)), but it is well established in various types of habitat: pine barrens, thick wooded undergrowth, wasteland and fields of rough grass, farmland, etc. Though edible, it is not systematically hunted or shot because the terrain is unsuitable for this form of sport and the birds are not concentrated in sufficient numbers in any one place.

Voice: the call note of the male is a loud, clear 'bob white' or 'bob whoit', heard from late March until August. Various other, sometimes human-sounding, whistles are made by members of a scattered covey to locate one another. The alarm note is a soft, continuous 'chipchupchipchup-chipchup'.

Nest: on the ground. Stated to lay 10 to 18 white eggs, but 10 is the largest number of young I have seen together. May–June seems to be the height of the breeding season.

RING-NECKED PHEASANT *Phasianus colchicus*   Pl 5; RTP 31
Status: NP: not found. Out Is: introduced round Hatchet Bay, Eleuthera (where seen 1959 (B-B)).
Description: male L 35″ (tail 18″); female L 21″ (tail 12″). This fine game bird is distinguished by its size and long, tapering tail alone. The male is richly coloured, the female mottled brown.

CHUKAR *Alectoris graeca* (English name: Rock Partridge)   Pl 5
Status: NP: not found. Out Is: introduced near Rock Sound, Eleuthera.
Description: L 13″ s A. A small, ground-dwelling bird, related and rather similar to the Bobwhite. It is brightly coloured, the white throat being the most noticeable feature. When flushed, rises with sudden, whirring flight.

LIMPKINS
Aramidae

LIMPKIN *Aramus guarauna*   RTP 21
Status: NP: RARE VAGRANT. Only twice recorded prior to 1962 (7 August 1960, 21 October 1961*). But in 1962 six birds were present during most of the year near St Augustine's Monastery, and others were regularly seen near Cable Beach. Not reported in subsequent years. Out Is: recorded from Inagua and Cay Lobos, and to be expected occasionally elsewhere as a vagrant.
Description: L 27″ s A. A large, odd-looking wading bird, reminiscent of a

heron or an ibis except for its long, pale, slightly decurved bill and speckled brown plumage. Limpkins feed on snails and so are not confined to the marshes and swamps that are their primary habitat: the Monastery birds frequented rocky, coppice-bordered fields.

RAILS, GALLINULES and COOTS
Rallidae

CLAPPER RAIL *Rallus longirostris*   Pl 5; RTP 22

Status: NP: FAIRLY COMMON RESIDENT. Out Is: recorded from most, and presumably found on all, main islands.

Description, habits: L 14″ s A. A large, skulking, *greyish marsh bird*, with a long, almost straight bill. The hind part of the body is barred grey and white and the stubby tail is white underneath, but the bird's shape and its *horizontal carriage* are more likely to be noticed. Clapper Rails are commonest in the swamps along the south and south-eastern coasts of New Providence (e.g. beyond the Prisons, Coral Harbour), where several birds may be heard calling at once. I have not seen them in the centre of the island, but they occur in smaller numbers on the northern part. Their known liking for salt water accounts for this, the tidal swamps being preferred to those that are merely brackish.

Voice: a loud 'kek kek kek kek kek kek kek kek'. This will be heard a dozen times for each time a clapper is seen.

Nest: stated to be on the ground, containing up to 9 buffy, brown-spotted eggs. Young are probably hatched in June.

SORA *Porzana carolina*   RTP 22

Status: NP: FAIRLY COMMON WINTER VISITOR. Arrives in October and leaves in early April. Extreme dates: 30 September, 15 April. Out Is: no doubt occurs throughout the Bahamas in winter, though not recorded from all islands.

Description, habits: L 9″ s A. Best distinguished by its *short, yellow bill* and skulking habits. Adults have brown upperparts, grey underparts, a *black face* and throat, and barred flanks. Immatures have pale-buff underparts and lack the black markings. Soras are elusive, swamp-dwelling birds that escape observation by running through thick grass or marsh vegetation. When flushed they rise with weak, fluttering flight and dangling legs, and drop into cover again immediately.

Voice: the alarm-note is a sharp 'keek'.

PURPLE GALLINULE *Porphyrula martinica*

Status: NP: UNCOMMON PASSAGE MIGRANT and occasional winter visitor. Occurs regularly in March, April, and May, and again from August to November. It would not be surprising if it remained to breed occasionally. Extreme dates: 3 March, 3 June; 21 July, 3 December. Also, exceptionally, 1–19 January. Out Is: very little data; no doubt occurs throughout the Bahamas on migration.

Description, habits: L 13″ S A. Adult plumage is deep *purple* on the head, neck, and underparts, and greenish on the upperparts (though these colours are not always apparent in poor light). Has a red and yellow bill, a light-blue frontal shield, white under tail-coverts, and *yellow legs*. Immatures are brownish, with yellow legs.

The beautiful Purple Gallinule is seldom seen in the open; it is a bird one flushes from some patch of reeds or surprises feeding in dense vegetation near water. It rarely swims, but climbs easily among reeds, and often flies to a tree when alarmed—all habits not shared by the next species.

Voice: the alarm-note is a rather effeminate, high-pitched cackling.

COMMON GALLINULE *Gallinula chloropus* (Other name: Florida Gallinule. English name: Moorhen)   Pl 5; RTP 22

Status: NP: COMMON RESIDENT. Out Is: presumably found throughout the Bahamas, though not recorded from all islands.

Description, habits: L 13″ S A. A medium-sized water bird, known by its *blackish plumage, red bill, and white under tail-coverts*. When alarmed it flicks its tail nervously and the flashing white feathers serve as a warning signal to its neighbours. The legs are green with a red garter, and there is a distinctive white line along the flanks. Common Gallinules are wary birds, and they run or swim for cover at the first sign of danger, often with loud cries of alarm. They are seldom seen flying, though if taken by surprise they will skitter along the surface of the water as far as the nearest patch of cover. They are found among mangroves and reeds, and on small ponds or along the edges of larger ones (not on open water like coot and scaup).

Voice: makes 'keeking', squawking, and other loud and raucous sounds.

Nest: usually a platform of reeds, on or near the water. The eggs, which may number up to 9, are buff with dark markings. The breeding season is from April to August.

AMERICAN COOT *Fulica americana*   Pl 5; RTP 22

Status: NP: COMMON WINTER VISITOR, UNCOMMON RESIDENT. Out Is: Surprisingly little data, but presumably occurs on all main islands.

Description, habits: L 15″ s A. Coot are *dark-grey, duck-like birds*, best identified by their *white bills*. The plumage is uniformly blackish-grey except for the white under tail-coverts and, in flight, a white line on the rear edge of the wings.

On New Providence, coot are most likely to be seen on Lake Cunningham, where they congregate in winter in 'rafts' of many hundred birds, often mixed with ducks. The main winter flocks arrive in November and December, and leave in March and April, but their dates of arrival and departure vary from year to year, no doubt according to weather conditions farther north. From May to late October (and particularly in August and September, when probably moulting) they become very scarce, only a few pairs remaining on small, secluded ponds.

Voice: coot make all sorts of sounds, some quite unbirdlike. The most common are 'werr' and 'wuk wuk wuk wuk wuk wuk wuk'.

Nest: normally a cup made of aquatic plants, placed on or near the water. As many as 10 or 12 eggs may be laid; they are buffish with dark-brown spots. I have only seen broods of 2 or 3 young successfully raised on New Providence.

OYSTERCATCHERS
Haematopodidae

AMERICAN OYSTERCATCHER *Haematopus palliatus* Pl 6; RTP 23, 27

Status: NP: not found. Out Is: resident on Andros, and from Exuma southwards. Also recorded from Abaco and Eleuthera, where probably vagrant.

Description: L 19″ s A. The *black-and-white pattern* (black head and neck, grey back, white underparts) and *long, red bill* identify this large shorebird. The legs are flesh-coloured. Stilts have red legs and a dark bill.

PLOVERS and TURNSTONES
Charadriidae

SEMIPALMATED PLOVER *Charadrius semipalmatus* (English name: Ringed Plover)

Status: NP: FAIRLY COMMON PASSAGE MIGRANT, UNCOMMON WINTER VISITOR. The main autumn passage takes place in September, tailing off in October. A few individuals remain all winter, and are joined by the spring migrants in late April and May. Extreme dates: 29 July, 3 June. Out Is: found throughout the Bahamas. Early date: Long Is, 17 July.

Description, habits: L 7″ s A. A small shorebird with *dark-brown* upperparts, and white underparts crossed by a dark breastband or collar. The stubby *bill and the legs are yellow* (but immatures have dark bills). Semipalmated Plovers frequent muddy beaches, as are found on the south side of New Providence, where they run swiftly and halt abruptly while searching for the small marine life they feed on. They are found singly or in small parties, sometimes mixed with Piping Plovers. On migration they are often found inland with sandpipers, usually by water but sometimes out on the grass on the golf courses.

Voice: a plaintive 'tooeee'.

PIPING PLOVER *Charadrius melodus*

Status: NP: RARE WINTER VISITOR. August (15th) to March (26th). There is an old July record. Out Is: only recorded from the northern islands, but to be expected occasionally throughout the Bahamas.

Description: L 7″ s A. A rare, pale relative of the preceding species, from which it is distinguished by its *pale*, sandy-coloured upperparts; from a distance it appears quite white. Its stubby bill and yellow legs preclude confusion with any shorebird except the Semipalmated. One year a party of about 10 Piping Plovers wintered at South Beach, but otherwise I have not seen them regularly. Careful examination of the whole south coast would probably reveal a few on migration or wintering every year.

Voice: a distinctive, piping 'peeplo' or 'peetoo'.

SNOWY PLOVER *Charadrius alexandrinus* Pl 6; RTP 24

Status: NP: not found. Out Is: a common breeding species, probably resident, on Gt. Inagua. Recorded from most of the southern Bahamas up to Exuma and San Salvador.

Description: L 6½″ s A. This is the palest of the small plovers, known by its *dark bill and legs* (yellow on the two preceding species). The dark 'collar' common to all these small plovers is reduced, on the Snowy, to two dark marks on the sides.

WILSON'S PLOVER *Charadrius wilsonia* (Other name: Thick-billed Plover)   **Pl 6; RTP 24**

Status: NP: FAIRLY COMMON SUMMER VISITOR; rare resident or winter visitor. Most Wilson's Plovers arrive in the second half of May and leave in late August and early September. They are quite rare from then until April, when the first migrants return. Out Is: found throughout the Bahamas in summer; status in winter uncertain.

Description, habits: L 7½″ s A. Wilson's Plovers have brown upperparts and white underparts, with a dark band crossing the breast. They have *stout, black bills*, and *flesh-coloured legs*. They are mostly found on the south side of New Providence, on and near the beaches. They escort human beings through their territories with great anxiety, running alongside the intruders until the invisible boundary of the next territory is reached, when another pair comes running up, calling anxiously, and the performance is repeated. When the young are hatched, families of Wilson's Plovers form groups of up to a dozen birds, but as soon as the young are fully grown the numbers begin to diminish, and soon only an occasional bird is found. This species, like most of our summer visitors, seems to leave as soon as it has completed its breeding cycle.

Voice: the commonest note is a loud 'wheep'.

Nest: a 'scrape' in the ground. Three pointed eggs, buffish with black markings, are laid in May or June. The young leave the nest soon after they are born.

KILLDEER *Charadrius vociferus*   **Pl 6; RTP 24, 28**

Status: NP: FAIRLY COMMON WINTER VISITOR. Arrives in October, becomes scarce during January, and finally disappears in March and April. Extreme dates: 4 October, 8 May*. Also late May and June records: see 'Nest'. Out Is: found throughout the Bahamas in winter. A local race is resident on Gt. Inagua and probably nests on other islands; there are June and July records from Andros and Cat Is respectively.

Description, habits: L 10″ s A. A large, noisy plover, distinguished by its size, habitat, and its *two black breast-bands*. It has brown upperparts, white underparts, and an orange-rufous rump and upper tail, noticeable in flight. Killdeer are found in small groups or in flocks of up to 50 birds, being particularly common on the golf courses; they run swiftly in search of insects, and fly round noisily when disturbed. In January their numbers diminish; at this time of year open grassland becomes very dry, which could account for their partial disappearance, but it seems more likely that most birds then leave for their breeding grounds, as the few that remain seem to be closely paired. They are then often found in mangrove swamps.

Voice: a loud, plaintive 'toeee' or 'queee'. Also 'tititititititoee', heard when birds take flight, and a trilling note, occasionally heard in winter but more typical of the breeding season.

Nest: the only record I have of this species between mid-April and October is of a single bird at Oakes Field, 28 May and 6 June 1960, which was trilling, doing elaborate injury-feigning, and showing the utmost anxiety as if it were nesting. Clearly, this species is a possible nester.

AMERICAN GOLDEN PLOVER *Pluvialis dominica*   RTP 24, 28
Status: NP: RARE PASSAGE MIGRANT. September (8th–24th). Out Is: very few records, but no doubt occurs from time to time on passage. Late date: Gd. Bahama, 23 November.
Description: L 10½″ s A. Similar to the Black-bellied Plover, but *smaller, darker*, and browner. In flight, *lacks the black axillars* and white wing and tail markings of the next species. In breeding plumage both this and the next species have largely black underparts. Golden Plovers have usually lost, or are in the process of losing, this plumage when they reach New Providence, but a variable amount of black may remain. Every autumn the Golden Plover undertakes a dramatic migration flight, travelling down the Atlantic, far from land, from Canada to South America. Individuals found in the Bahamas are likely to be stragglers from the migrating flocks or near-victims of hurricanes. Exceedingly rare in the spring, when the main line of migration is through Central America.

BLACK-BELLIED PLOVER *Squatarola squatarola* (English name: Grey Plover)   RTP 24, 28
Status: NP: common winter visitor. Non-breeding birds are fairly common in summer and the species is therefore PRESENT ALL YEAR ROUND. Out Is: found throughout the Bahamas.
Description, habits: L 12″ s A. *A stout, grey shorebird* with a short bill. In flight it shows an infallible field-mark: *black axillars* (the axillars are equivalent to the human armpit). In breeding plumage the underparts are

Plate 5

Plate 6

jet-black, bordered on the sides of the head and throat with white, the back remaining grey as in winter. This striking plumage is seen on New Providence for only about two months of the year, for although it is grown in April and not lost till October, the breeding birds in question leave by mid-May and do not return until mid-August or September.

Black-bellied Plovers are particularly common on muddy beaches at low tide, running swiftly here and there, and flying from one place to another with loud, whistling calls ('tlee-oo-wee'). Also found by ponds and on golf courses.

RUDDY TURNSTONE *Arenaria interpres* (English name: Turnstone)
RTP 25, 28

Status: NP: fairly common winter visitor. Non-breeding birds are also fairly common in summer, so the species is PRESENT ALL YEAR ROUND. Out Is: found throughout the Bahamas.

Description, habits: L 8″ s A. A stocky, medium-sized shorebird with a rufous back, white underparts, patterned black-and-white head and breast, and orange legs. In flight it shows a remarkable black-and-white pattern on the upperparts. Winter and immature plumages are browner and more drab than the breeding plumage (and an intermediate plumage is common), but the *distinctive flight pattern* is always retained.

Turnstones are found in groups of from 2 to 20 birds, 4 or 5 being an average number. They feed industriously among the seaweed and other flotsam on the high tide mark of sandy beaches, but prefer rocky or muddy beaches such as those on the south side of New Providence. I have occasionally found them inland when on passage, once turning over clods and digging unconcernedly in a ploughed field.

SNIPE and SANDPIPERS
Scolopacidae

COMMON SNIPE *Capella gallinago* (Formerly Wilson's Snipe. English name: Snipe)
RTP 25, 29

Status: NP: FAIRLY COMMON WINTER VISITOR. Arrives in October and leaves again by mid-April. Commonest, some years, in November and December, before flooded land starts drying, thereafter becoming progressively scarcer, but this is not noticeable in wet winters. Extreme dates: 21 September, 2 May. Out Is: no doubt occurs throughout the Bahamas in winter, though not recorded from all islands.

Description, habits: L 11″ s A. Known by its disproportionately *long*, *straight bill* and brown, beautifully patterned plumage. Snipe are seldom seen on the ground on account of their protective colouring, but suddenly fly up in front of one, with a rasping note, and make off with fast, zig-zagging flight. They are usually found singly or in twos and threes, though I have seen as many as 14 together. They are commonest on the edges of ponds or in mangrove swamps, but are found even in thick woodland if there are a few boggy patches.

WHIMBREL *Numenius phaeopus* (Formerly Hudsonian Curlew)

RTP 23, 27

Status: NP: RARE. Apparently an occasional passage migrant with non-breeding individuals sometimes present in summer. May (29th); July (31st) to October (1st). Out Is: Hardly any records, but no doubt occurs sparingly on migration.

Description: L 16½" s A. The Whimbrel is a *large, brown shorebird* with a *long, curved bill*. The plumage is dark-brown on the upperparts, paler-brown on the underparts, and there are two dark stripes on the head. The Whimbrel's main migration route is stated to lie across the sea to the east of the Bahamas (e.g. N. Carolina to Brazil) so one should look for it on the more easterly islands or after hurricanes.

UPLAND SANDPIPER *Bartramia longicauda* (Former names: Bartram's or Bartramian Sandpiper, Upland Plover)

RTP 23, 30

Status: NP: UNCOMMON AUTUMN MIGRANT, RARE SPRING MIGRANT. The autumn migration extends from August to early October, most records being for the first half of September. There are very few spring records. Extreme dates: 11 April, 10 May*; 1 August, 10 October*. Also, exceptionally, 1 December*. Out Is: presumably found throughout the Bahamas on migration. Early spring date: Bimini, 4 April.

Description, habits: L 12" s A. Best identified by a combination of characteristics: small head, shortish bill, thin neck, fat-looking body, and long tail. The underparts are buffish and the upperparts brown, beautifully marked with dark streaks and speckles. The neck is usually cinnamon-coloured and the legs yellowish or greenish. Upland Sandpipers are found in ones and twos (and once a party of 4) on such few grassy spaces as exist on New Providence, feeding on insects, which are caught with a quick, darting movement of the head. They are rather wild.

SPOTTED SANDPIPER *Actitis macularia*   RTP 26, 29

Status: NP: FAIRLY COMMON PASSAGE MIGRANT, RARE WINTER VISITOR.
Autumn passage lasts from late July to December, and a few individuals
remain all winter. The spring passage is in April and May. Extreme dates:
8 July, 3 June. Out Is: found throughout the Bahamas.

Description, habits: L 7½″ s A. A small, plain sandpiper with brown upperparts and white underparts. From April to August most birds are more or
less spotted with black on the underparts. Best identified by two characteristics: on the ground by its *constant 'teetering'*, the tail and body moving
up and down all the time (a habit shared by the waterthrushes), and, in
flight, by the *short, irregular wingbeats* with the wings held below the level
of the body. Spotted Sandpipers are usually found in ones and twos, on
beaches or by the edges of ponds and pools, and sometimes out on the
grass among Bobolinks, running nimbly here and there in pursuit of
insects. They are very numerous at the height of the spring passage, in
May, and then sometimes occur in unlikely places far from water.

Voice: a loud, clear 'peet-weet'.

SOLITARY SANDPIPER *Tringa solitaria*   RTP 25, 29

Status: NP: FAIRLY COMMON PASSAGE MIGRANT, RARE WINTER VISITOR.
The autumn passage extends from late July to December, and an occasional
bird remains all winter. The spring passage begins in March, but is most
noticeable in April and May. Extreme dates: 24 July, 20 May. Out Is:
found throughout the Bahamas.

Description, habits: L 8½″ s A. The Solitary Sandpiper is about half-way in
size between the two species it most nearly resembles: the Spotted Sandpiper and the Lesser Yellowlegs. It has dark-brown upperparts, white
underparts, a *pale eyering*, and long, *greenish legs*. The dark tail has a
white 'herringbone' pattern on each side, noticeable in flight. The Solitary
Sandpiper is found feeding on the edges of pools or wading in shallow
water, bobbing its head when nervous, but usually flying only a short
distance when disturbed. It is, as its name suggests, a rather solitary bird,
although small groups are sometimes seen, and it commonly associates
with Spotted Sandpipers.

Voice: a loud, clear, 'peet weet' or 'peet weet weet', similar to the Spotted
Sandpiper's call. Also 'pit pit pit' when alarmed.

WILLET *Catoptrophorus semipalmatus*   Pl 6; RTP 25, 30

Status: NP: UNCOMMON PASSAGE MIGRANT and vagrant. Occurs annually in April (and May*), and irregularly in autumn and winter. One July record. Out Is: a common resident on most islands. Some southward movement in winter is to be expected.

Description: L 15″ s A. A long-legged, long-billed wader, with greyish plumage; except for its bluish legs it resembles a large yellowlegs. In flight the bold *black-and-white* undersurface of the wings becomes visible; this is an unmistakable field-mark. Though relatively common on many out islands, Willets occur more or less accidentally on New Providence. They frequent mudflats, mangroves, and edges of ponds.

GREATER YELLOWLEGS *Totanus melanoleucus* RTP 25

Status: NP: FAIRLY COMMON PASSAGE MIGRANT, less numerous in spring than in autumn. A few non-breeding individuals are found during every month of the year. Out Is: found throughout the Bahamas.

Description: L 14″ s A. Distinguished from the commoner Lesser Yellowlegs (q.v.) by its *greater size*, more orange-yellow legs, and longer, slightly upturned bill. Found by ponds, in swamps and flooded land, and sometimes on coastal mudflats, usually in ones and twos, though parties of 4 or 6 (paired birds?) appear in the spring.

Voice: a loud, clear 'tew tew tew' or 'tew tew tew tew'. See following species.

LESSER YELLOWLEGS *Totanus flavipes* (English name: Yellowshank)
RTP 25, 29

Status: NP: COMMON AUTUMN AND UNCOMMON SPRING MIGRANT; rare winter visitor. The main autumn passage is from August to November, but stragglers are found all winter, particularly in cold winters. Spring passage is in the second half of April and in May. Extreme dates: 7 July, 29 May. Out Is: found throughout the Bahamas. Early date: Bimini, 2 July.

Description, habits: L 10½″ s A. Known by its *long, lemon-yellow legs.* The upperparts are grey and the underparts white, the bill *thin and straight.* In flight, the uniform upperparts (no wing markings) and white rump and tail are distinctive. Yellowlegs are almost always found by water, where they wade briskly, picking insects off the surface. They are noisy and easily alarmed; when nervous they jerk their heads up and down and, if danger continues to approach, fly round calling, often only to settle again close by and resume jerking their heads anxiously. The present species is found in ones and twos, or up to about 5 birds together, sometimes with Greater Yellowlegs and often with smaller sandpipers.

Voice: both Yellowlegs have a loud, clear call, typically repeated twice by the Lesser and three or four times by the Greater. Either species, when alarmed, calls an indefinite number of times, but usually reverts to type at the end of the series, as: 'tew tew tew tew tew tew tew, tew tew, tew tew'.

PECTORAL SANDPIPER *Erolia melanotus*   RTP 26, 30

Status: NP: FAIRLY COMMON AUTUMN PASSAGE MIGRANT. There is a steady passage from August to October, diminishing in November and virtually ceasing by the middle of that month. I have not seen this species in spring, when it is stated to be a rare migrant. Extreme dates: 31 July, 6 December. Out Is: found throughout the Bahamas on autumn passage.

Description, habits: L 9″ s A. Similar to a Least Sandpiper in plumage, with brown upperparts, white underparts, brown streakings forming a 'bib' on the upper breast, and yellow legs. However the Pectoral is distinguished from the Least, and indeed from most of the confusing sandpiper tribe, by its *size*, for it is half as large again as Leasts, Semipalmateds, etc., and nearer in size to Killdeer and Black-bellied Plovers.

Pectoral Sandpipers are sociable birds, and keep close together in flocks which may number 5 or 6 birds or, on a 'big day', 50 or 100. They may be found anywhere by the edges of pools and ponds, but on New Providence are commonest on Lyford Cay golf course, where they feed on insects on the greens and fairways.

Voice: A grating 'trrirp, trrirp'.

WHITE-RUMPED SANDPIPER *Erolia fuscicollis*   RTP 26, 30

Status: NP: only one record: 15 May. Evidently an OCCASIONAL PASSAGE MIGRANT. Out Is: seldom recorded, but occurs on migration. Extreme dates: Inagua, 27 May; Bimini, 17 August; Gd. Bahama, 3 October.

Description: L 7½″ s A. Similar to Least or Semipalmated Sandpipers except for its larger size, longer bill, and *white rump*, visible in flight. To be looked for among flocks of other small waders.

Voice: a distinctive 'zeet', unlike other sandpiper calls.

LEAST SANDPIPER *Erolia minutilla*   RTP 26, 30

Status: NP: COMMON PASSAGE MIGRANT, RARE WINTER VISITOR. The autumn migration starts in late July and continues to the end of October. Thereafter scarce, but a few individuals remain all winter. Spring migration is during the last half of April and in May. Extreme dates: 17 July, 29 May. Out Is: found throughout the Bahamas. Early date: Long Is, 16 July.

Description, habits: L 6″ s A. The smallest of its family, the Least Sandpiper has brown upperparts, white underparts with brown markings on the upper breast, forming a 'bib', and *yellowish legs*. Frequently found with Semipalmated Sandpipers, which are greyer-plumaged and black-legged but otherwise similar. Least Sandpipers are found in loose flocks by the muddy margins of pools, where they run swiftly to and fro, feeding on insects and tiny aquatic life. Also found on the golf courses and muddy beaches. Tame.

Voice: a shrill 'treep', when disturbed.

DUNLIN *Erolia alpina* (Other name: Red-backed Sandpiper)

RTP 24, 26, 30

Status: RARE WINTER VISITOR. August (10th) to April (15th). The August date appears to be an exceptional one: Dunlins are not to be expected much before November. Out Is: no reliable records.

Description: L 8½″ s A. A relatively large, chunky sandpiper, known in winter plumage by its plain grey back, *dusky upper breast*, and fairly long bill, *decurved* at the end. The legs are short and black. The distinctive low-pitched, rasping call note, uttered when flushed, and, in flight, the narrow white line along the wings are also helpful points. Though rare so far south, Dunlins will probably be found to be regular winter visitors to the northern Bahamas. I have five separate records of from 1 to 3 birds, mainly at South Beach.

DOWITCHER *Limnodromus griseus* (A.O.U. list name: Short-billed Dowitcher. Former English name: Red-breasted Snipe)   RTP 25, 29

Status: NP: FAIRLY COMMON AUTUMN PASSAGE MIGRANT, RARE WINTER VISITOR, UNCOMMON SPRING MIGRANT. The main passage is from August to October. One or two small parties remain all winter, and are rejoined by the few spring migrants in April and May. Extreme dates: 22 July, 3 June. Out Is: found throughout the Bahamas on passage and sometimes in winter.

Description, habits: L 12″ s A. Heavily built, greyish birds with *very long, straight bills*. In flight they show a wedge-shaped area of *white on the rump and lower back*. The underparts are reddish in breeding plumage, notably in April, May, August, and September, but many individuals remain in non-breeding plumage, so the average flock at that time of year contains both grey and reddish birds. Dowitchers are usually found in groups of 2 or 3 up to about 20 birds, often, on coastal mudflats, with Black-bellied Plovers and smaller waders or, inland, with yellowlegs. They feed, like snipe, by plunging their bills vertically into the mud. Rather tame.

Voice: a clear, ringing 'tew tew tew', similar to the call of a Yellowlegs.

STILT SANDPIPER *Micropalama himantopus* RTP 25, 29

Status: NP: RARE PASSAGE MIGRANT. May (13th); July (31st) to November (1st). Out Is: very little data; no doubt occurs on most islands occasionally. Early and late autumn dates: Inagua, 18 July; Gd. Bahama, 20 November.

Description: L 8½″ S A. Similar in flight pattern and general appearance to a Lesser Yellowlegs, the Stilt Sandpiper is distinguished, in winter plumage, by its longer bill, greenish legs, and pale stripe over the eye. In breeding plumage the underparts are heavily barred, and the cheeks are crossed by a *rust-coloured stripe*. Migrants may be in breeding, winter, or intermediate plumage.

SEMIPALMATED SANDPIPER *Ereunetes pusillus* and WESTERN SANDPIPER *Ereunetes mauri* RTP 26, 30

Status: NP: COMMON AUTUMN MIGRANTS, RARE WINTER VISITORS, FAIRLY COMMON SPRING MIGRANTS. The autumn passage is in August, September, and October, a few birds passing later and some remaining all winter. The spring passage is principally in May. Extreme dates: 29 July, 6 June. Out Is: found throughout the Bahamas. Early dates: Inagua, 23 July (Semipalmated), 24 July (Western)

Description, habits: L 6¼/6½″ S A. These two species are so similar that it is seldom possible to tell them apart in the field. They are small 'mud-birds' with greyish upperparts, white underparts, and *black legs*. The main difference between them lies in the bill: a typical Semipalmated has a short, straight bill, a typical Western has a longer, plainly decurved one. The Western is a slightly larger bird and sometimes, in early autumn, shows some reddish feathers on the back. The Semipalmated is the commoner of the two.

Found on the edges of pools, on mud beaches and golf courses, these active little sandpipers are rather pugnacious, always fighting among themselves and bullying the smaller Leasts, with which they commonly associate. Tame.

SANDERLING *Crocethia alba*   RTP 26, 29

Status: NP: UNCOMMON WINTER VISITOR. November (21st) to March (4th). Out Is: found sparingly throughout the Bahamas in winter. Extreme dates: Harbour Is, 9 November; Exuma, 4 April (B-B).

Description, habits: L 8″ s A. Distinguished from other small sandpipers by its much *whiter plumage* and straight, black bill and legs. The upperparts are pale-grey, the underparts so white as to be noticeable half a mile away. Larger and paler than Semipalmated Sandpipers, Sanderlings show a black mark on the shoulder and, in flight, a long, white line along the wings.

They are most easily seen at low tide, when they frequent the seaward edge of the half sandy, half muddy beaches on the south-eastern part of the island. They are found singly or in parties of 5, 10, or 25 birds, frequently with other shorebirds. Not seen inland.

BLACK-NECKED STILT *Himantopus mexicanus*   Pl 6; RTP 23, 27

Status: NP: FAIRLY COMMON SUMMER VISITOR. Arrives in April and leaves early in September. Extreme dates: 24 March, 24 September. Out Is: found virtually throughout the Bahamas in summer. Extreme dates: Inagua, 20 March; Eleuthera, 11 November.

Description, habits: L 14″ (legs 9″) s A. Stilts are known by their black upperparts, white underparts, and *disproportionately long, red legs*, which in flight extend far beyond the tail. They are very noisy, especially near their nests. They are found in small parties (of up to 14 birds) during April, and gradually split up into pairs. After the breeding season they are mostly found in family groups, when the young can be identified by their browner upperparts and paler legs. Stilts feed on aquatic insects in mud or shallow water, notably on the edges of mangrove swamps, and are occasionally seen on golf courses when these are flooded. These beautiful and harmless birds have suffered greatly from shooting in the past, and deserve strict protection.

Voice: a loud, incessant 'wit wit wit wit wit', when alarmed.

Nest: though elsewhere they commonly nest in loose colonies, on New Providence each pair usually nests separately. A slight nest of twigs and stones is made on some muddy islet, but if heavy rain causes the surrounding water to rise (as frequently happens), the birds build a veritable mud-castle to protect the eggs. Four buff-coloured eggs, marked with black, are laid. Stilts are bold in defence of their nests.

GULLS and TERNS
Laridae

HERRING GULL *Larus argentatus*   RTP 5, 6
Status: NP: UNCOMMON WINTER VISITOR. October (8th) to May (21st).
Most records are for October, November, and December. Out Is: apparently occurs regularly in the northern Bahamas in winter, and irregularly farther south, but there is surprisingly little data available.
Description, habits: L 25″ s A. *The largest gull* found in the Bahamas. I have recorded only immature Herring Gulls (see under Laughing Gull for description); adults evidently do not venture so far south. This is the least common of the winter gulls, and it stays the shortest time, as only stragglers are found beyond the end of December. Normally from 1 to about 6 birds will be found together (once 20), often with larger numbers of their smaller relatives. They seem to confine themselves to the coast between Rock Point, opposite the Grove Estate, and Nassau port, coming to shelter on Big Pond when there is a strong north wind.

RING-BILLED GULL *Larus delawarensis*   RTP 5, 6
Status: NP: FAIRLY COMMON WINTER VISITOR. First becomes numerous in December, and mostly leaves by the end of March. Extreme dates: 13 October, 13 May. Out Is: very little data, but apparently occurs regularly in the northern Bahamas in winter, and irregularly farther south.
Description, habits: L 19″ s A. This is our *medium-sized* gull, smaller than a Herring Gull, larger than a Laughing Gull. The dark ring on the bill distinguishes it from the Laughing but not from the Herring, which is also ring-billed. See under Laughing Gull for description. Ring-billed Gulls are chiefly found along the 3½-mile stretch of coast from Nassau port to Rock Point, though they are also fond of inland waters. They are found singly or in small parties, alone or with other gulls, the largest number I have seen together being about 30.

LAUGHING GULL *Larus atricilla*   Pl 6; RTP 5, 6
Status: NP: FAIRLY COMMON RESIDENT. Out Is: found throughout the Bahamas.
Description, habits: L 6½″ s A. This is the *smallest* of the three gulls normally found round New Providence, and is the only one *found in summer*. At that time of year the *black head* makes identification doubly easy, but this becomes white from about September to March.

In winter, not only are two other species of gull present, but each species is found in two different plumages, giving a total of six apparently different gulls. Their differences are:

Herring, 1st yr. imm.: large, ring-billed, uniformly dark-brown.

Herring, 2nd yr. imm.: large, ring-billed, pale-brown upperparts, white underparts, mostly dusky tail.

Ring-billed, imm.: medium size, ring-billed, brown upperparts, white underparts, white tail with a thin black band.

Ring-billed, adult: medium size, ring-billed, light-grey upperparts, white underparts.

Laughing, adult (winter): small size, plain dark bill, dark-grey upperparts, white underparts.

Laughing, imm.: small size, plain dark bill, dark-brown upperparts, white underparts but with brown breast, white tail with black band.

Laughing Gulls, though resident, vary their habitat very markedly, sometimes being found by scores in and near the port and sometimes being totally absent except during storms. It is during the summer that they frequent the vicinity of the port; they appear suddenly in April, often wheeling and soaring over the town with loud cries, and they disappear almost as abruptly in September. Storms bring them to the port again, or to the West Bay Street coast, and they sometimes come to land in fine weather, but on the whole are seldom seen in winter. The Nassau colony of Laughing Gulls numbers rather over 100 birds. The only time, in winter, that I made an accurate count there were 142.

Voice: Though supposedly a laughing cry, from a distance it is more of a continuous miaouing sound, most often heard when a party circles high overhead. Noisy in April and May.

Nest: in colonies on the ground. I do not know where the 'Nassau colony' nests. Stated to lay 2 or 3 olive-coloured eggs, blotched with brown. Probably laid in May and June.

GULL-BILLED TERN *Gelochelidon nilotica* Pl 7; RTP 7, 8

Status: NP: FAIRLY COMMON SUMMER VISITOR. Arrives at the end of April and leaves in August, as soon as the young are fully fledged. Extreme dates: 15 April, 24 September. Out Is: found throughout the Bahamas in summer. Extreme dates: Inagua, 21 March; Gd. Bahama, 12 November.

Description, habits: L 14″ S A. Known by its pale-grey upperparts with a black cap, white underparts, and *stout, black bill*. The only other summer tern on New Providence is the smaller, yellow-billed Least Tern. Gull-billed Terns *habitually feed over land*: they are seen in ones, twos, and small parties, hawking with strong, graceful flight over mangroves, coppice, scrub, golf courses, airports, lakes, and even over partially built-up areas of Nassau. Large insects are caught, and sometimes the males present them with much ceremony to the females; I have also seen lizards and frogs being carried.

Voice: a loud 'kak-ak, kak-ak-ak' and 'kawak'. This frequently draws attention to birds flying over.

Nest: I have failed to locate the nests or nesting colony of this species, but young birds appear in July and August.

COMMON TERN *Sterna hirundo*   RTP 7, 8

Status: NP: RARE VAGRANT, recorded in June and July. Out Is: very little data. Occurs on passage and in the summer months; will perhaps be found to nest.

Description: L 15″ S A. The Common Tern is in fact not one of the common terns in the Bahamas. Similar in plumage to other terns, it is distinguished in summer by its *red bill* with a black tip. See following species. Common Terns seem to appear off the coast of New Providence accidentally; it is difficult to account for their presence in summer as they are not known to nest near by.

Voice: 'Kee-arr', stated to be a good way of distinguishing Common from Roseate Terns.

ROSEATE TERN *Sterna dougallii*   Pl 7; RTP 7, 8

Status: NP: recorded in August* and September*. Presumably a RARE VAGRANT or passage migrant. Out Is: common off many islands in summer, nesting on small cays. Status in winter uncertain; perhaps a summer visitor only.

Description: L 15½″ S A. Though basically similar to many other terns, with a black cap, grey upperparts, and white underparts, the Roseate is a paler, *whiter-looking* bird than its relatives, and has longer tail-feathers. Typically, *the bill is black*, or black with a little red at the base, but this is variable and some individuals have mainly red bills like Common Terns. However the colour of the bill remains the most obvious field-mark and can be used with reasonable certainty in summer if a sizeable flock is seen.

Voice: one of the call notes is a soft, un-ternlike 'chuick'.

SOOTY TERN *Sterna fuscata* (Local name: Egg Bird)   Pl 7; RTP 9
Status: NP: not likely to be seen from land, but is found in nearby waters and nests on a cay within sight of NP. Out Is: a summer visitor, nesting in colonies on small cays and rocks, often with Bridled and Noddy Terns.
Description: L 16″ s A. A tern of the open sea, with *uniformly black upper-parts* and a long, forked tail. Underparts white, bill black. Immatures have brown plumage, speckled with white on the back, and could be confused with Noddies at a distance.

BRIDLED TERN *Sterna anaethetus* (Local name: Egg Bird)   Pl 7
Status: NP: not likely to be seen from land, but is found in nearby waters. Out Is: a summer visitor, nesting in colonies on small cays and rocks, often with Sooty and Noddy Terns.
Description: L 15″ s A. A dark-backed tern of the open sea, likely to be confused with the Sooty. The Bridled Tern is distinguished by its *whitish collar* (or bridle) dividing the black cap from the *greyish-brown back*. The long, forked, white tail is also noticeable. Underparts white, bill black.

LEAST TERN *Sterna albifrons* (English name: Little Tern) Pl 7; RTP 7, 9
Status: NP: FAIRLY COMMON SUMMER VISITOR. Arrives in early May and leaves in August as soon as nesting is over. Extreme dates: 30 April, 13 September. Out Is: found throughout the Bahamas in summer. Early date: Andros, 19 March.
Description, habits: L 9″ s A. The Least Tern, like others of its family, has grey upperparts, white underparts, and a black cap. It is distinguished by its *small size* and *yellow bill*. Least Terns usually nest at Coral Harbour and Lyford Cay (but absent in 1962). Though commonest in the vicinity of their nesting colonies, single birds or small groups will forage at some distance from their nests; they are often seen not far offshore, or over inland waters, plunging into the water after fish, usually hovering briefly before plunging.
Voice: a sharp 'kik, kik', a rasping 'chizeek', and other calls. Very noisy in the vicinity of the nest.
Nest: a simple 'scrape' on the ground. Two, sometimes 3, buff-coloured eggs marked with black and dark-brown are laid. The scattered colonies, which are not necessarily by the coast, may consist of only a few birds or, on New Providence, up to about 30 pairs. I once found an absolutely isolated nest on the edge of the road to South Beach. Nesting starts in May, soon after arrival, and would be completed in two months but for

misfortunes, of which the local colonies have a fair share. Very fierce in defence of the nest.

ROYAL TERN *Thalasseus maximus*   Pl 7; RTP 7, 8
Status: NP: UNCOMMON WINTER VISITOR. September (1st*) to May (28th). Out Is: found throughout the Bahamas, breeding on small cays. Relatively common on some islands (e.g. Bimini) perhaps owing to the proximity of suitable nesting sites.
Description, habits: L 19½″ s A. A *large* tern, as big as a small gull. It has grey upperparts, white underparts, black head-feathers (of varying extent according to the time of year) which stand out in a sort of shaggy crest, and a large, *orange bill*. The Royal is most often seen fishing close offshore or resting on some convenient pole. Only a few birds are found round New Providence, mostly off the south and west coasts, usually in ones, twos, or threes.
Voice: a loud 'kreer'.

SANDWICH TERN *Thalasseus sandvicensis* (Other name: Cabot's Tern)
                                                                       Pl 7; RTP 7, 8
Status: NP: RARE VAGRANT. Recorded 7 and 9 March, and 17 June†. Out Is: Surprisingly little data. Common on some islands (e.g. Bimini) but apparently absent from others. Breeds on small cays. Perhaps a summer visitor only.
Description: L 15″ s A. A fairly large, maritime tern, best identified by its long, *black bill, tipped with yellow*. The plumage is otherwise similar to that of most terns: grey upperparts, white underparts, and a black cap in the breeding season. This species is among the many seabirds that are more or less common on other islands but that rarely frequent the coast of New Providence; I have only recorded it after a severe gale. To be looked for in the port.

BLACK TERN *Chlidonias niger*   RTP 7, 9
Status: NP: RARE PASSAGE MIGRANT. August (19th) to September (13th). Out Is: Not many records, but occurs on migration, presumably throughout the islands. Spring date: Inagua, 11 April; early autumn date: Inagua, 25 July.
Description: L 9½″ s A. Late summer migrants are already in 'winter' plumage, with dark-grey upperparts, white underparts, and a small, *dark cap* on the back of the head; this is divided from the dark feathers of the back by a *white collar*. The *small size* and thin, black bill are also helpful

points. In breeding plumage (in spring) the head and underparts are black. Black Terns are found singly over inland water, hawking with graceful, buoyant flight and picking insects off the surface.

NODDY TERN *Anoüs stolidus* (Local name: Egg Bird)   Pl 7; RTP 9
Status: NP: not likely to be seen from land, but is found in nearby waters and nests on a cay within sight of NP. Out Is: a summer visitor, nesting in colonies on small cays and rocks, often with Bridled and Sooty Terns.
Description: L 15″ s A. The uniform *dark-brown* plumage, both on the upper- and underparts, and the *whitish cap* distinguish the Noddy from other pelagic terns. However the pale cap is not particularly noticeable at a distance and should be looked for, as immature Sooty Terns are also brown-plumaged. The tail of the Noddy is rounded; other terns have forked tails.

SKIMMERS
Rynchopidae

BLACK SKIMMER *Rynchops nigra*   RTP 9
Status: NP: one picked up dead on beach, 9 February*; otherwise not recorded. Out Is: recorded from Bimini (March, April), Gd. Bahama (December), and Inagua, being no doubt a vagrant to these and other islands.
Description: L 18″ s A. The black upperparts, white underparts, and long, *red bill* distinguish this seabird at a distance; the *projecting lower mandible* (longer than the upper mandible) precludes any doubt at closer range. Often flies low over the sea with the lower mandible slicing through the water ('skimming').

PIGEONS and DOVES
Columbidae

WHITE-CROWNED PIGEON *Columba leucocephala*   Pl 9; RTP 60
Status: NP: UNCOMMON. Mainly a winter visitor (September–May), but also recorded in summer. May still nest in small numbers. Out Is: found throughout the Bahamas; often common. Nests in colonies on small cays. Shot in great numbers on certain islands, particularly Andros.
Description, habits: L 13½″ A *large, dark,* square-tailed pigeon with a *white crown.* The crown is brilliant white on males. but whitish on females

Plate 7

Plate 8

1. **Yellow-billed Cuckoo**   page 69
   Rufous wing-patch. Pure white underparts
   (partly ochre on Mangrove Cuckoo).

2. **Barn Owl**   72
   Large; white; nocturnal.

3. **Burrowing Owl**   73
   Small; brown; partly diurnal.

4. **Northern Mockingbird**   89
   Grey, unstreaked plumage. White wing-markings and
   edges of tail.

5. **Hairy Woodpecker**   78
   White back and underparts; speckled wings. Voice.

6. **Common Nighthawk**   74
   Pointed wings with white patch. Fast, erratic flight.
   Voice.

and greyish on immatures. Even when the colour of the crown cannot be clearly seen—and this is frequently the case when a bird dashes unexpectedly out of a tree—a *wild* pigeon with uniform dark-grey plumage can be no other species.

White-crowned Pigeons are mostly found in thick, jungly coppice where it is difficult to do more than glimpse an occasional bird. When disturbed, they fly with clattering wings, but as they fly low over the coppice and settle again close by, they seldom gain enough height to be clearly visible. On out islands they are commoner and perhaps less persecuted than on New Providence, and are more often seen flying about.

ZENAIDA DOVE *Zenaida aurita*   Pl 9
Status: NP: RARE RESIDENT. Out Is: found throughout the Bahamas, being common on most islands.
Description, habits: L 11″ s A. A handsome dove with brown upperparts and an orange-pink head and underparts. A bluish sheen on the neck and black spots on the wing are noticeable at close quarters. In flight, the *white line* along the rear edge of the wing and the *square, white-tipped tail* are distinctive. Zenaida Doves feed on the ground and fly to a tree when alarmed, often allowing one to take a good look (or a well-aimed shot) from close by. They are distinctly rare on New Providence, presumably because of excessive human persecution. On out islands, they often frequent coppice and open country; on New Providence mostly pine barrens.
Nest: stated to nest in trees and bushes, or on the ground, laying 2 white eggs.

WHITE-WINGED DOVE *Zenaida asiatica*   Pl 9
Status: NP: not found. Out Is: recorded only from Gt. Inagua, where rare or uncommon, and once (14 November) from Gd. Bahama.
Description: L 11″ s A. Easily identified in flight by the broad white line that crosses the inner part of each wing; this is noticeable even at a distance. The rounded tail has two white patches.

MOURNING DOVE *Zenaidura macroura*   Pl 5; RTP 40
Status: NP: UNCOMMON RESIDENT. Out Is: probably found throughout the Bahamas, though not yet recorded from Acklins, Crooked Is and Mayaguana. Common on certain islands (e.g. Eleuthera).
Description, habits: L 12″ s A. Distinguished from other pigeons by its *long, pointed tail*, bordered with white. The plumage is brownish on the

upperparts, and pinkish on the underparts. Mourning Doves feed on the ground, often in high, weed-ridden grass, but are most frequently seen in the air, where their swift flight and graceful form are distinctive. Scarce on New Providence, no doubt due to excessive persecution. Single birds, pairs, and an occasional flock are seen from time to time, 27 birds being the largest number that I have seen together. My records show them to be most numerous between August and November, but round St Augustine's Monastery, where they are relatively common, no seasonal fluctuation is noted.

Nest: the only nest I have found (in June) was in a young pine, about 20 ft. up. A small platform serves for a nest, and 2 white eggs are laid.

GROUND DOVE *Columbigallina passerina* (Local name: Tobacco Dove)
Pl 5; RTP 40

Status: NP: ABUNDANT RESIDENT. Out Is: common resident on all islands.
Description, habits: L 6¾″ Ground Doves look like what they are: *half-sized pigeons*. Their best field-mark is the patch of *rufous on the wings*, noticeable when they fly. Males can be distinguished by the blue-grey sheen on their heads and by their pinkish underparts from the paler females. Ground Doves are very tame, unconcernedly running out of the way of a passing car or pedestrian, and taking flight only at the last possible moment. They feed on the ground, taking seeds, and run and walk with bobbing heads, like true pigeons. They are found in pairs throughout the year, but groups of 10 or 20 birds congregate where food is plentiful. They are very aggressive and can spoil the pleasure of having a bird-table, as they drive off the smaller birds and fight tirelessly among themselves.
Voice: a soft, repeated cooing which, except at close quarters, sounds like a rhythmic 'wook, wook, wook, wook, wook'. Heard steadily from January to September, and infrequently thereafter.
Nest: builds a small cup-shaped nest of twigs or casuarina needles, placed from 3 to 40 ft. up in the fork of a branch or close against the trunk of a tree—frequently, on New Providence, a casuarina. The 'eaves' of palm trees are another favourite place. A number of pairs sometimes nest close together. Two white eggs are laid; the breeding season extends from March to September, reaching a peak in April and May.

WHITE-BELLIED DOVE *Leptotila jamaicensis*   Pl 9
Status: NP: UNCOMMON RESIDENT. Out Is: not found.
Description, habits: L 12½″ S A. A relatively dull-plumaged pigeon, with

brown upperparts and a *white face and underparts*. The White-bellied Dove frequents the same type of country as the quail-dove, and has the similar habits of feeding rather noisily among fallen leaves and of being off in a flash at the first sign of danger. This species was introduced from Jamaica as part of the programme to restock the island with birds after the hurricanes of the late '20s. It is hard to imagine a worse choice from the point of view of the general public, because the number of people who see this species each year can surely be counted on the fingers of one hand. It ranks with the quail-dove as our most elusive bird.

Nest: stated to be similar to that of a Zenaida Dove.

KEY WEST QUAIL-DOVE *Geotrygon chrysia*   Pl 9

Status: NP: FAIRLY COMMON RESIDENT. Out Is: found only on Andros, Gd. Bahama, Abaco, and Eleuthera.

Description, habits: L 11″ S A. A handsome pigeon with warm, rufous upperparts and pale, buffish underparts. It has iridescent green and purple head- and neck-feathers, a coppery patch on the shoulders and top of the back, a red beak and eyering, and flesh-coloured legs. The best field-mark on the ground, however, is the broad, *white line across the face*. In flight, and the bird is usually seen briefly and in flight, the *fox-red* colour of the upperparts is immediately noticeable, and the general pigeon shape, like an outsize Ground Dove, is helpful.

This elusive bird lives on the floor of impenetrable tracts of coppice, but when feeding it sometimes comes out on to a path or track, where with luck one can get a good view of it. It sometimes draws attention to itself by the rustling sounds it makes among the dry leaves of the coppice floor, but then it usually walks or runs away from the intruder and takes flight silently on reaching an open space. If surprised, however, it flies with clattering wings. Though typical of the wilder parts of the island, quail-doves come to within a stone's throw of houses, and are frequently seen from a car as they fly across the road from one tangled wall of trees and undergrowth to the other.

Voice: The 'song', heard from January to early September, is a curious, mournful 'ooooou', repeated a number of times, reminiscent of the sound of wind in an empty bottle.

Nest: stated to nest in undergrowth or on the ground, laying 2 buff-coloured eggs.

PARROTS
Psittacidae

CUBAN PARROT *Amazona leucocephala*　　　　**Pl 9**
Status: NP: not found. Out Is: resident only on Abaco (a few) and Gt. Inagua. Was also found until recently on Acklins.
Description: L 12″ s A. *The only parrot* of the Bahamas. The plumage is mainly green, with a white forehead, red throat, and partly blue wings.

CUCKOOS and ANIS
Cuculidae

MANGROVE CUCKOO *Coccyzus minor* (Other name: Black-eared Cuckoo)　　　　**Pl 10; RTP 60**
Status: NP: FAIRLY COMMON RESIDENT. Out Is: recorded from almost all main islands.
Description, habits: L 12″ s A. A long-tailed bird with brownish upperparts and white underparts, except for the thighs and posterior underparts which are *cinnamon-coloured*. It has a more or less distinct black mark on the cheek, the lower mandible is yellow, and the tail is marked with black and white.

The commonest of its family, the Mangrove Cuckoo does not inhabit mangroves on New Providence. It is typical of almost impenetrable, jungly coppice, but is not averse to more open wooded country (other than pinewoods), nor to the vicinity of houses, but its infrequent movements among the foliage rarely attract attention. It is a tame and rather sluggish bird.
Voice: a loud 'ka-ka-ka-ka-ka-ka-ka-ka-ka-ka-kow-kow-kowp', the last notes being partially 'swallowed', and inaudible from a distance. The call is shorter and delivered more slowly than that of the lizard cuckoo. Young birds beg with a feeble 'kew-kew-kew'.
Nest: stated to build a nest of twigs at low elevations, laying 2–3 greenish-blue eggs. Probably lays in May or June.

YELLOW-BILLED CUCKOO *Coccyzus americanus*　　　　**Pl 8; RTP 40**
Status: NP: A SUMMER VISITOR in the region of St Augustine's Monastery*. My few records of this species are for April, May, October, and November, so it is no doubt also a passage migrant. Extreme dates: 12

April, 4 December*. Out Is: probably occurs throughout the Bahamas, either as a migrant or a summer visitor, though not recorded from all islands.

Description: L 12″ s A. Very similar to the Mangrove Cuckoo, but with *pure white underparts* (partly cinnamon on the Mangrove) and a *rufous* patch on the *wings* (lacking on the other species). This rufous patch is particularly noticeable in flight. Both species have a yellow lower mandible and a long tail with black-and-white markings. The Yellow-billed Cuckoo, the rarer of these two closely related species, is slimmer and rather more active than the Mangrove Cuckoo, and flies more readily. Inhabits coppice and woodland.

Voice: rather similar to the preceding species.

Nest: stated to be similar to the preceding species.

BLACK-BILLED CUCKOO *Coccyzus erythropthalmus*   RTP 40

Status: NP: RARE PASSAGE MIGRANT. Recorded only three times: September (9th*) to October (23rd*). Out Is: recorded only from Gd. Bahama, 15 November. To be expected occasionally on most islands on migration.

Description: L 11½″ s A. Distinguished from the preceding species by the *black bill*, thin red ring round the eye, lack of rufous on the wings, and relative lack of white on the tail. By far the rarest cuckoo.

GREAT LIZARD CUCKOO *Saurothera merlini* (Formerly Cuban Lizard Cuckoo)   Pl 10

Status: NP: FAIRLY COMMON RESIDENT. Out Is: found only on Andros and Eleuthera (including Harbour Is).

Description, habits: L 20″ s A. An unusual bird of ungainly appearance, sluggish habits, and remarkable tameness. The upperparts are brownish-grey with some rufous on the wings, the underparts are whitish except for the thighs and under tail-coverts, which are ochre. The tail is very long, from below white crossed with black bars. There is a patch of red skin round the eye, and the large bill and legs are horn-coloured. Its *size* alone is near double that of our other cuckoos, but the *red eye-patch* in conjunction with the partly ochre underparts provides a supplementary means of identification.

Great Lizard Cuckoos inhabit thick, jungly country—the thicker the better. This may be high or low coppice, or undergrowth in wooded country, so long as it is virtually impenetrable. Here they feed mostly on the ground, moving with a fast, shuffling run. They also feed in low trees and bushes, but I believe that often when they are found at this height it is because they have heard one approaching. They climb small trees with some facility, hopping and clambering about in quite a lively manner, though the length of their tail sometimes makes it difficult for them to turn round. They are incapable of sustained flight and indeed appear to be unable to fly in a horizontal direction at all. Normally they climb to some little height and then fly downwards to the next tree, climb up it, then fly down again to the next one, and so on.

These cuckoos are so absurdly tame that they will allow one to approach to within two paces of them, when they adopt odd, parrot-like defensive postures. When much molested, they curse with loud, harsh cries, and sometimes seem to lose all self-control, flying hysterically this way and that, thrashing about in the trees, and making strange screaming noises. They feed on insects and lizards. I saw one catch a medium-sized lizard, beat it about, and swallow it whole, and another appeared to be picking at the cells of a wasps' nest. Lizard cuckoos are not likely to be seen at all frequently, but they can be heard from many different points on the island, which suggests that they are widely distributed in suitable terrain.

Voice: a loud, rapid 'ka-ka-ka-ka-ka-ka-ka-ka-ka-ka', faster and longer sustained than the Mangrove Cuckoo's comparable call. Also a croaking 'cra-cra-cra', a loud 'ack-ack-ack', and various other discordant cries.

Nest: stated to lay 2 or 3 white eggs at low or moderate elevations above the ground. Breeding probably starts in May.

SMOOTH-BILLED ANI *Crotophaga ani* (Local name: Crow)

Pl 10; RTP 60

The name perhaps comes from the Latin *anilis* = old-womanish.

Status: NP: COMMON RESIDENT. Out Is: resident on all main islands.

Description, habits: L 14″ (tail 7″) S A. This is one of the few birds that most Nassau residents are familiar with. It is known by its uniform coal-black plumage, long tail, and large, high-ridged bill.

Anis are found in noisy flocks of 6 to 16 birds, 10 or 12 being an average number. They fly one behind the other with weak, flapping flight, and when the leading bird lands in a tree, all the others pile in on the same branch or crash-land near by, all the time emitting their raucous cry. Though ungainly, they are by no means foolish, for a sentinel is always stationed to keep watch while the rest of the flock is feeding. They feed on or near the ground in thick grass, low brush, etc., and sometimes in the open, where they run and hop surprisingly fast. They sometimes get rather dispersed, but it is exceptional to see an Ani which does not prove, on investigation, to form part of a flock. When resting they commonly perch close up against one another, and are fond of preening the neck-feathers of their neighbours, parrot-fashion. After rain or after taking a bathe, they 'hang themselves out to dry' in the most uncouth postures, lying on the ground with outspread wings and even, it is said, hanging upside down from a branch. Their food is mostly insects, notably small moths, but lizards are regularly taken and frogs occasionally. Their usual habitat is open country and fields of rough grass, but they are also found in scrub, woods, coppice, mangroves, and gardens. Not uncommon in Nassau.

Voice: the usual note is a loud, repeated 'kwaylieek'.

Nest: A large, open cup of sticks and twigs, lined with leaves, the few that I have seen being 6–10 ft. up in mangroves. The eggs are chalky blue. Several females use the same nest, 20 or more eggs having been recorded in several layers in one nest. The breeding season seems to extend round the whole year.

OWLS
Strigidae

BARN OWL *Tyto alba*   **Pl 8; RTP 38**

Status: NP: UNCOMMON RESIDENT. Out Is: recorded from most main islands.

Description, habits: L 17″ S A. *A large, pale, nocturnal owl.* The upperparts are orange-brown, beautifully patterned, and the underparts mostly white. This species, like all owls, has binocular vision, which gives it an impressive 'human' appearance, accentuated by its large, heart-shaped face.

During the day Barn Owls sleep in buildings or thick, leafy trees; by night they search for food with silent, ghostly flight, and appear to be pure white. It is difficult to form an accurate estimate of the commonness of this species, for they are seen daily in some places (near their nesting sites?) while in other places one may go for months or years without seeing one. I think that there are relatively few pairs on New Providence, and that most of them are concentrated in the Nassau area.

Voice: hissing and other unbirdlike noises, including a wild shriek. More often heard than seen.

Nest: in cavities or buildings. A pair at St Augustine's Monastery nests during the second half of the year, laying as many as 8 eggs. The eggs are white.

BURROWING OWL *Speotyto cunicularia*   **Pl 8; RTP 39**

Status: NP: FAIRLY COMMON RESIDENT. Out Is: recorded from most, but not all, main islands.

Description, habits: L 9″ *A small, diurnal owl*, often seen on the ground. The plumage is *brown*, spotted and streaked with white, particularly on the underparts. During the breeding season, Burrowing Owls are usually seen standing at the entrance of their burrows, singly or in pairs. On being approached they bob nervously up and down, chatter at the intruder, and finally scuttle down their burrows or fly a short way with their typical bounding flight. Outside the breeding season they are often found perched in trees or old buildings, presumably sleeping, for they seem to revert to more nocturnal habits at that time of the year.

Large insects are their main food but, judging by the left-overs round their burrows, many frogs and an occasional mouse or bird are taken; presumably lizards are also eaten. On one occasion I watched young birds toying with a piece of food which turned out to be the leg of this same species; Brother Ignatius Dean has similar evidence of cannibalism.

Voice: 'cucking' and chattering noises of alarm and anger. The song is a high 'coo-co-hoo'.

Nest: at the end of a longish burrow, which the birds (females only?) dig for themselves, usually in sandy soil. The entrance is littered with rubbish of all sorts: paper, cigarette packets, seaweed, horse-droppings, etc. Several pairs often nest close to one another in loose colonies, but others nest alone. 7 or 8 pairs used to nest on and near Cable Beach golf course, but their burrows were destroyed or stopped so often that the colony was abandoned after the 1960 season. A single pair has now (1963) returned. But there are 3 or 4 other nesting places in the Cable Beach area, 1 or 2 at Lyford Cay, several near St Augustine's Monastery, and no doubt many on other parts of the island. Digging starts in December and January, the young appear at the mouths of their burrows in May, and the burrows are abandoned in July.

NIGHTJARS
Caprimulgidae

CHUCK-WILL'S-WIDOW *Caprimulgus carolinensis*   **RTP 40**

Status: NP: UNCOMMON WINTER VISITOR. September (20th) to April (17th), but the bird is so seldom seen that it may well be present before and after these dates. Out Is: recorded only from Andros, Gd. Bahama, and

Gt. Inagua, but no doubt occurs on most islands in winter. Late date: Andros, 15 May.

Description, habits: L 12″ A brown, mothlike, nocturnal bird, related to the nighthawk. It is *larger* and *browner* than a nighthawk (some individuals are distinctly reddish; nighthawks are always greyish) and is further distinguished by being *round-winged* and round-tailed, strictly nocturnal, and a winter visitor. White markings on the tail distinguish males from females.

While a nighthawk flying in the dusk can be seen outlined against the sky, the Chuck-will's-widow flies low over the ground, invisible against a dark background. In the daytime it remains hidden in thick woodland, and it requires luck more than anything else to flush one. In my 4½ years on New Providence I have only once had a good view of a perched bird in full daylight.

Voice: calls regularly at dusk in March. From a distance the call sounds like 'kwéeeoo, kwéeeoo' (or weel's weedow!). There is no similar bird call at night on New Providence. Occasionally imitated by Mockingbirds.

COMMON NIGHTHAWK *Chordeiles minor*   Pl 8; RTP 40

Status: NP: ABUNDANT SUMMER VISITOR. Arrives in the last week of April and usually leaves by mid-September, after which only presumed migrants and stragglers are seen. Extreme dates: 6 April*, 8 November. Out Is: common in summer throughout the Bahamas. Late date: Gd. Bahama, 14 November.

Description, habits: L 9″ Nighthawks may be seen in great numbers on summer evenings, hawking with *swift, erratic* flight. The unusual way they fly and their *distinctive call* (see 'Voice') makes them easily identifiable. The plumage is a mottled and barred brownish-grey, so inconspicuous as to make a bird on the ground almost invisible. Males have white throats and white markings on the tail, lacking on females, but both sexes have a white patch on their *long, pointed wings*.

Nighthawks feed exclusively on flying insects; Mr Pough in his Audubon Guide mentions one whose stomach contained 2,175 flying ants and another that had taken over 500 mosquitoes; these figures always heighten my pleasure when watching the birds feeding. Although they belong to a family of nocturnal birds, nighthawks may be seen at any time of day, rain in particular causing them to take to the wing. Normally, however, they appear an hour or two before sunset.

Aerial display starts soon after arrival and continues till the end of July; in it the male swirls down from high in the air almost to the ground, and rockets up again, its feathers at the bottom of the dive making a sound like tearing linen. This may be done again and again at half-minute intervals, and is interesting to watch. Nighthawks are common over Nassau and over all types of country.

Voice: the call is a loud 'pity-pit-pit', usually repeated at frequent intervals and accompanied by a more rapid movement of the wings, as if keeping time with the call. They call from the time they arrive until August, when they become almost silent.

Nest: no nest is made, the eggs being deposited on the ground, usually in a gravelly or stony place. I have seen a nest in the middle of a little-used road. The eggs are oval and of a blue-grey colour, marked with blackish and purply speckles; normally laid in May or June. Only one egg is usual on New Providence, though 2 out of 12 nests examined contained 2 eggs. Young birds can run quite well, balancing themselves on their wings, and at an early age may move a few yards from the original nesting site.

Note: the species described above is the so-called Cuban Nighthawk (*C.m.gundlachii*), but a North American form (*C.m.minor*) is found in the Bahamas on migration. It is indistinguishable in the field except for its totally different call-note: a weak, grating 'pee-eent'. This is heard infrequently from among the earlier arrivals (11–25 April) over New Providence. There is no doubt a return passage in October, but both sub-species are then silent.

HUMMINGBIRDS
Trochilidae

EMERALD HUMMINGBIRD *Chlorostilbon ricordii*   **Pl 12**

Status: NP: OCCASIONAL VAGRANT. Recorded 23 November 1967†, and once previously, many years ago. Out Is: common resident on Andros, Gd. Bahama, and Abaco only.

Description: L 4¼″ The male is known by its *mainly green plumage* (including the throat), while females are distinguished from female woodstars by their forked, instead of rounded, tails and *lack of rufous* on the underparts. This is a larger species than the next, and the call is quite different—a metallic 'tchiw, tchiw'.

BAHAMA WOODSTAR *Calliphlox evelynae* (Local name: Hummingbird)
     Pl 12

Status: NP: ABUNDANT RESIDENT. Out Is: resident on all main islands, apparently being relatively uncommon on Gd. Bahama and Abaco (and Andros?), where the preceding species is found.

Description, habits: L 3½″ This is, to all intents and purposes, *the only species of hummingbird on New Providence* and on most of the out islands. It has greenish upperparts, a white chest, and *rufous* lower underparts. Adult males have iridescent *violet throat-feathers* which are strikingly beautiful when seen flashing in the sunlight, but which appear black when seen from a distance, in poor light, or from an unfavourable angle. Females and immatures (which greatly outnumber adult males) have white throats and are a disappointment to people who expect all hummingbirds to be brightly coloured. Males have a forked tail, females a rounded one. Immature males when changing plumage have greyish throats, often with a few violet spots.

Woodstars are common wherever there are flowers: in gardens, woods, coppice, or open country. When feeding, they hover in front of each flower in turn, maintaining themselves stationary on wings that move so fast as to be invisible, and probe for nectar and minute insects. Less commonly they hawk for midges in the air. Though a number of them may gather where flowers are abundant, they are not sociable birds and will chase an intruding neighbour away—this aggressiveness being shown towards other species at times. When resting, they like to perch on an exposed twig, or sometimes a telephone wire, and will allow one to approach to within a few feet. At all times, in fact, they show indifference to the presence of human beings.

A distinct local race, or sub-species, of the Bahama Woodstar is found on the Inaguas, males of which have violet feathers on the forehead as well as on the throat.

Voice: the usual note is a staccato 'tit, titit, tit, tit, titit', often speeded up into a rapid, rattling sound such as a dwarf kingfisher might make. Usually made in flight, occasionally when perched. The song is a dry, rhythmic sound, not unlike that of a fisherman's reel, which I have noted as 'prítitidee, prítitidee, prítitidee'. It is most often heard during the beautiful courtship display, but single birds will sometimes sing to themselves while perched.

Nest: the well constructed nest is little more than one inch in diameter, and is round, open, and made of a soft, woolly material similar to thistledown, camouflaged on the outside with tiny pieces of bark. A variety of sites are used, the nests that I have seen being from 2 to 12 ft. up in trees or bushes, usually in or on a fork in the twigs. Two rather elongated white eggs are laid. Breeding takes place all year round, but the main season is in April.

Note: Ruby-throated Hummingbirds (see Appendix) are often erroneously reported in the belief that a 'red-throated' hummingbird must be of that species. The misunderstanding arises because the throat-colour of the male woodstar varies according to the position of the viewer and the angle of light; from certain angles it throws a distinctly red flash. Ruby-throated Hummingbirds are best distinguished by the lack of rufous on their lower underparts.

KINGFISHERS
Alcedinidae

BELTED KINGFISHER *Megaceryle alcyon* RTP 54

Status: NP: COMMON WINTER VISITOR. Arrives in August and leaves again in April, a few birds being found, however, all through the year. June records are the most unusual: I have only three, the 1st, 17th, and 21st, in different years. Out Is: found throughout the Bahamas.

Description, habits: L 12″ Known by its *heavy bill, crested head,* large size, and, above all, by its *habits.* The upperparts are blue-grey, the underparts white crossed by a grey breastband, females having an additional 'belt' of a rufous colour.

Kingfishers frequent seacoast, mangrove swamps, lakes, ponds, and flooded land, and perch on some favourite rock, branch, or wire, from which they plunge into the water after fish. They are also seen hovering above the water or flying with irregular wingbeats between different points in their territory. Angry chases often take place, particularly when kingfishers just arrived from the north come trespassing on the preserves of earlier arrivals.

Voice: A loud, distinctive rattle, somewhat like a toy machine-gun. A noisy bird.

WOODPECKERS
Picidae

WEST INDIAN RED-BELLIED WOODPECKER *Centurus superciliaris*
Pl 10

Status: NP: not found. Out Is: resident on Gd. Bahama, Abaco, and San Salvador only. Uncommon.

Description: L 10½″ Known by its heavily *barred, black and white back* and wings, and *red belly*. Males also have the entire crown and nape red, females the nape only. (The two following species may show some red on the head, but never on such an extensive area.)

YELLOW-BELLIED SAPSUCKER *Sphyrapicus varius*   RTP 41

Status: NP: COMMON WINTER VISITOR. Arrives in early November and leaves in March. Extreme dates: 17 October, 15 April. Out Is: found throughout the Bahamas in winter. Early date: Gd. Bahama 14 October, and an unusual summer record from Acklins: 22 July.

Description, habits: L 8½″ This woodpecker is best identified by the *long white stripe* on the closed wing. Adults have a distinctive black-and-white pattern on the head and a *red* patch on the forehead and, in males, on the throat. However most birds seen are in immature plumage which is brown and nondescript except for the wingstripe.

The sapsucker is a tame and rather noisy bird, most often noticed as it flies from one tree to another with the bounding flight characteristic of woodpeckers. Clinging to the treetrunks it bores parallel rows of holes in the bark, from which it takes sap and the insects attracted by the sap. It is found wherever there are trees (though scarce in pine-woods), and is common in inhabited areas.

Voice: Cat-like mewing notes and various chattering sounds.

HAIRY WOODPECKER *Dendrocopos villosus*   Pl 8; RTP 41

Status: NP: FAIRLY COMMON RESIDENT (in spite of reports to the contrary). Out Is: resident on the pine-forested northern islands: Andros, Gd. Bahama, and Abaco.

Description, habits: L 9″ A predominantly *black and white* bird, distinguished from the preceding species by its pure white underparts (yellowish, buffish, on the sapsucker) and speckled wings (lacking the sapsucker's wingstripe). Adult males have a bright *red patch* on the back of the head; young males show some red on the forehead. This is the only species of woodpecker on New Providence during the six summer months.

Though found mainly in the pine-woods during the breeding season, Hairy Woodpeckers wander into other wooded areas at other times of year, sometimes feeding in tall trees, but as often on a low branch among undergrowth or on a small sapling close to the ground. Their principal food is stated to be the larvae of wood-boring insects, and these they uncover in true woodpecker style, clinging, often vertically, to a tree or branch and hammering with amazing force. They keep together in pairs all through the year and are best located by their distinctive call.

Voice: a loud 'keek'; also a conversational chattering sound. There is no song; this function is replaced by 'drumming' with the beak on a resonant branch. I have heard this peculiar sound from March to July.

Nest: in a cavity bored in a tree, frequently a dead tree or a palm. Four white eggs are stated to be the normal clutch; they are laid from March onwards.

TYRANT FLYCATCHERS
Tyrannidae

EASTERN KINGBIRD *Tyrannus tyrannus* RTP 42

Status: NP: UNCOMMON AUTUMN AND RARE SPRING MIGRANT. April (9th–11th); August (30th) to October (15th*). Out Is: few records; no doubt occurs occasionally on migration on all islands. Early spring date: Cat Cay, 6 April.

Description: L 8¾″ s A. Distinguished from other flycatchers by its *blackish* upperparts, contrasting white underparts, and *white-tipped tail*. It is a smaller, smarter-looking bird than the common Grey Kingbird, and perches with more upright stance and flies more gracefully. This is an abundant species in North America, including Florida, in summer, but it is surprisingly uncommon in the Bahamas.

GREY KINGBIRD *Tyrannus dominicensis* (Local name: Fighter)

Pl 11; RTP 65

Status: NP: ABUNDANT SUMMER VISITOR. Grey Kingbirds arrive in the second half of April and are common everywhere by the end of the month. Their numbers diminish during August, and by the end of September all the local birds have left. During the whole of October, however, a stream of migrants passes over Nassau, apparently in a south-easterly direction, and small groups stop and feed for a few hours before moving on. Extreme dates: 31 March, 12 November. Out Is: common in summer throughout the Bahamas. Late date: Gt. Inagua, 12 December.

Description, habits: L 9¼″ s A. This is an *all-grey* bird, dark on the upper-parts and pale on the underparts, with a *heavy bill*, *broad tail*, and pointed wings. There is no white in the plumage. Grey Kingbirds feed on insects, mostly large ones, which they catch on the wing. For this purpose they choose exposed perches—television aerials, tops of royal palms, telephone wires, bare branches—from which they make rapid sallies. Large insects

Plate 9

Plate 10

1. **West Indian Red-bellied Woodpecker**   page 77
   Barred back and wings; red head and belly.
   Gd. Bahama, Abaco & S. Salvador.

2. **Great Lizard Cuckoo**   70
   Large size; red eye-patch; ochre tail-coverts.
   New Providence, Andros, Eleuthera.

3. **Mangrove Cuckoo**   69
   Black eye-line; ochre tail-coverts. Plain wings
   (rufous on Yellow-billed Cuckoo).

4. **Smooth-billed Ani**   71
   All-black; big bill; long tail.

5. **Red-legged Thrush**   91
   Grey plumage; red legs and eye-ring; white-tipped tail.

6. **Bahama Mockingbird**   90
   Streaked flanks; white-tipped tail. (Further distinguished
   from Northern Mockingbird by brown plumage and
   lack of white wing-markings.)

7. **Pearly-eyed Thrasher**   91
   Pale eye and bill; heavily streaked underparts.
   Absent northern islands.

such as dragonflies and cicadas are carried back to the perch and there hammered into submission and swallowed; in the meantime, however, the victims make loud buzzing and other sounds which appear to come from the kingbird itself. In Nassau some enterprising birds feed at night, catching the insects that swarm round the street-lights. Berries are sometimes taken. The kingbird's habitat is varied: gardens, roadsides, open woodland, edges of pine-woods, mangrove swamps, and streets of Nassau.

Grey Kingbirds are exceedingly aggressive, and attack everything that enters their territory or violates their airspace: men, dogs, and birds from the size of the Great Blue Heron downwards. They seldom, if ever, strike a man or a dog, but will often knock feathers from a bird. They are strong fliers and very quick on the wing. When migrating or flying any distance the flight is distinctively uneven, as they beat their wings a number of times, then 'miss a beat' by closing the wings. Except during the latter part of their stay, they are very noisy: they sing after a fashion, they call constantly, and birds of a pair salute one another each time they meet, which is several hundred times a day. Readily identified by their voice alone.

Voice: call and alarm note: a loud 'pitírre' or 'pitchirée'. The song, mostly heard at dawn and dusk, is a musical variation of the call, each phrase having at least six syllables and a certain rhythm: 'pitiréee, pitírrio', and 'peterpee petchurry', constantly repeated. At the nest a conversational trilling 'pritititititit' is often heard.

Nest: a flimsy construction of twigs, often lined with grasses, placed at varying heights in trees, especially pines and palms, in mangroves, and in odd positions such as on the crossbar of a steel lamp-post. Two to 4 eggs are laid, typically in June, but I have not known more than 2 young to be raised successfully. The eggs are pink, boldly marked with purple and brown, especially round the thick end. Kingbirds are fierce in defence of the nest.

LOGGERHEAD KINGBIRD *Tyrannus caudifasciatus* (Formerly Loggerhead Flycatcher)   **Pl 11**
Status: NP: FAIRLY COMMON RESIDENT. Out Is: resident on the pine-forested northern islands: Andros, Gd. Bahama, and Abaco.
Description, habits: L 9¼″ s A. Loggerhead Kingbirds are the same size as Grey Kingbirds, but substantially larger than Stolid Flycatchers. Their plumage is brownish on the upperparts, with a *dark cap* down to the level of the bill, and whitish on the underparts except for the more or less *yellow under tail-coverts*. In summer they are easily confused with Grey Kingbirds,

chiefly because the Greys are then so common, but Loggerheads are distinctly browner, and the brown tail with a thin, whitish line at the tip is a useful mark in flight.

Loggerhead Kingbirds are found in all types of woodland, often sitting rather quietly on a branch at medium height and making infrequent sallies after their insect prey. Berries are sometimes taken, and were fed to the young in the nest I watched, and I have seen lizards killed and swallowed. In late spring this species virtually disappears from a large part of its range and retires to the pine-woods, where it evidently holds its own against the more aggressive Grey Kingbird. The Loggerhead's distribution in the Bahamas suggests that pine-woods are essential to its survival, though in winter, in the absence of the other species, any type of woodland suits it well. Loggerhead Kingbirds are rather less common than Stolid Flycatchers, but much commoner than the Greater Antillean Pewee, thus ranking first in size but second in commonness among our three resident flycatchers. Silent and rather solitary birds outside the breeding season.

Voice: the call is a loud, churring 'teerrrp'. A series of similar notes: 'teerrr, teerrr, teerrr' is heard during courtship and when angry. The song, seldom heard, is a bubbling 'ppirriuppirriuppirriu'.

Nest: the only nest I have seen was indistinguishable from that of a Grey Kingbird. It was 25 ft up a pine tree, loosely constructed of twigs, and contained young in July.

WESTERN KINGBIRD *Tyrannus verticalis* (Formerly Arkansas Kingbird)
RTP 42

Status: NP: RARE PASSAGE MIGRANT. March (16th*); October (15th) to November (1st*). Out Is: recorded from Bimini, Gd. Bahama, and Eleuthera (late date: 26 November), and no doubt occurs occasionally on other islands on migration.

Description: L 9″ S A. This kingbird has a *grey head* and chest and a *yellow belly*. The tail is black with a thin, white lateral border. The only other flycatcher with such extensively yellow underparts is the still rarer Great Crested Flycatcher (see Appendix), which is distinguished by its rufous tail. As its name implies, the Western Kingbird inhabits the western part of the USA, but it strays regularly to the east coast on autumn migration, and will probably prove to be a regular visitor to the Bahamas.

STOLID FLYCATCHER *Myiarchus stolidus*   Pl 11
Status: NP: FAIRLY COMMON RESIDENT. Out Is: resident on the pine-

forested northern islands of Andros, Gd. Bahama, and Abaco, and apparently irregularly distributed farther south, being known from the Berry Is, Eleuthera, the Crooked/Acklins group, and Gt. Inagua.

Description, habits: L 7½″ s A. Noticeably smaller than the Loggerhead Kingbird, noticeably larger than the Greater Antillean Pewee, the Stolid Flycatcher has brown upperparts and white or whitish underparts. The best field-marks are its dark-brown cap, confined to the top of the head, and the partly *rufous tail-feathers*, noticeable in flight. The plumage is rather variable, as a few birds have the under tail-coverts sufficiently yellow as to be noticeable in the field (like Loggerhead Kingbirds), while others, particularly young birds, have unusually bright rufous markings, both on the tail and on the wings. But see 'Voice'. Stolid Flycatchers are found in pine-woods, mixed woodlands, and high coppice, and are the commonest of the resident flycatchers. They are active birds and make constant sallies after insects, also feeding regularly on berries, which they pick while hovering; once observed killing a lizard. They normally choose perches at medium height, but there is no strict vertical division of habitat between the flycatchers.

Voice: the call note is a loud, emphatic 'wheep'—an invaluable aid in first identifying the species. It is mostly heard from November to May, especially in the spring when it is sometimes repeated 8 or 10 times a minute. A variety of notes are heard during the breeding season: a bold 'teerr, teerr', like the Loggerhead's note, a quiet 'quip, quip, quip', and snatches of song, which include a whistled 'trahee, trahee'.

Nest: stated to nest in holes in trees, laying 3 or 4 eggs. Nesting seems to take place in April and May, chiefly in the pine-woods.

ACADIAN FLYCATCHER *Empidonax virescens*   RTP 110

Status: NP: once collected, 14 October 1961*. See below. Out Is: recorded from Cay Lobos and Gd. Bahama. No doubt occurs on most islands on migration.

Description: L 6″ s A. It is difficult to distinguish this small flycatcher from the Greater Antillean Pewee, and virtually impossible to distinguish it from certain other North American flycatchers. However it is the only one of its group that is *known* to occur here, having been collected, and it is the most likely to be found on migration as it winters in South America. Compared with our resident Greater Antillean Pewee, the neater plumage, whiter underparts, more strongly marked wingbars, rounder eyering, stronger flight, and choice of more conspicuous perches and more open habitat, are all minor but helpful points suggesting the present species.

When a small rush of flycatchers of this type comes through—I have noted them in the second half of September—one can only assume that they are Acadians.

GREATER ANTILLEAN PEWEE *Contopus caribaeus*   **Pl 11**
Status: NP: UNCOMMON RESIDENT. Out Is: resident on the pine-forested northern islands: Andros, Gd. Bahama, and Abaco; evidently fairly common in some places. Also recorded from Eleuthera and Cat Is.
Description, habits: L 6¼″ S A. This is the smallest of our three resident flycatchers and, although only 1¼″ in length separate it from the commoner Stolid Flycatcher, its *diminutive size* is immediately noticeable. The plumage is dull-brown on the upperparts and buffish on the underparts, sometimes with a trace of yellow down the centre of the breast. Some birds have a slightly crested appearance, others have grey feathers on the rump and lower back, but the best field-mark is the *pale eyering*, which broadens out behind the eye. Instead of forming the conventional circle round the eye, the ring is virtually invisible in front and plainly visible behind the eye— a minor but distinctive feature.

Pewees are usually seen singly, sitting with upright posture on some low branch or twig, or making quick sallies after passing insects. On returning to their perch after a sally the tail is briefly shivered; this is characteristic. They are very tame. Such inconspicuous birds may well appear to be less common than is really the case; they are often found on the edges of the pine barrens, and are probably fairly numerous in that almost impenetrable habitat. During the second half of the year they are found in all types of wooded country, but by February they withdraw again to the pine barrens, and can be looked for in vain on the rest of the island during the next six months. This confirms what their distribution in the Bahamas already suggests, namely that this species is dependent on pine woods as a breeding habitat.
Voice: the song is a clear, ringing 'peeee, dee-dee-dee-dee-dee', with the 'dees' on a descending scale. Call note: 'peewee' or 'peeweeoo'.
Nest: stated to be a small cup in a tree, containing 2 to 4 eggs, often with markings forming a wreath round the middle of the egg.

SWALLOWS
Hirundinidae

BAHAMA SWALLOW *Callichelidon cyaneoviridis* **Pl 11; RTP 60**
Status: NP: UNCOMMON. Principally a summer visitor. Passage birds
arrive in March and local birds in April, the latter disappearing abruptly
at the end of July. Some migrants are noted thereafter and there are winter
records, mostly old ones. Out Is: known to nest on Andros, Gd. Bahama,
and Abaco. Found, or to be expected, on other islands on migration or in
winter.
Description, habits: L 6″ s A. The Bahama Swallow has greenish upperparts (brown on immatures) and pure white underparts, the green feathers
appearing merely to be dark and of no particular colour except at close
quarters. It is distinguished from the very similar Tree Swallow by its
deeply forked tail, like that of a Barn Swallow.

Bahama Swallows are distinctly uncommon on New Providence: I know
of only two places where they can be seen at all regularly. One is round the
British Colonial Hotel and on West Bay Street to below Fort Charlotte,
where a small party is found each summer. This group certainly nests on
the hotel building some years and probably does so every year, their
presence here being interesting because they have been found in this
vicinity since 1859. The other place is towards the southern end of Gladstone Road where a flock of some 20 birds is present most summers, presumably nesting in the nearby pine woods. Clearings in pine woods are
their normal habitat. This species is known only from the Bahamas, Cuba,
and Florida, and its breeding range is apparently confined to the northern
Bahamas.
Voice: a metallic 'chep' or 'chi-chep'.
Nest: stated to nest in holes in trees or woodpiles, or under the eaves of a
building, laying 3 white eggs.

TREE SWALLOW *Iridoprocne bicolor* **RTP 43**
Status: NP: UNCOMMON PASSAGE MIGRANT. Seen regularly from August
to November, the main passage being in September and October. A less
marked passage takes place in the spring, mainly in February. I do not
believe that this species (nor any swallow) winters on New Providence,
though there are records from December (2nd†) and January (28th†). Out
Is: seldom recorded, but must occur on passage on most islands.
Description, habits: L 5½″ s A. Very similar to the preceding species, with
metallic greenish-blue upperparts (brown on immatures) and pure white

underparts, but distinguished by its relatively *square* tail as compared with the deeply forked tail of the Bahama Swallow. This distinction is quite plain when the birds are well seen, particularly when they fly overhead, but the two species are often indistinguishable when seen fleetingly or at a distance. Flocks of Tree Swallows join forces with other migrant swallows in autumn, and mixed flocks of 3 or 4 different species are not uncommon.

BANK SWALLOW *Riparia riparia* (English name: Sand Martin) RTP 43
Status: NP: UNCOMMON PASSAGE MIGRANT. April (14th*) to June (3rd); August (23rd) to October (22nd*). Most numerous in September. Out Is: no doubt found sparingly throughout the Bahamas on migration. Early autumn date: Gd. Bahama, 14 August.
Description: L 5¼″ s A. A small, *brown-backed* swallow whose white underparts are crossed by a *dark chest-band*. Very few are seen on New Providence, usually in ones and twos, often accompanying parties of Barn Swallows.

ROUGH-WINGED SWALLOW *Stelgidopteryx ruficollis*   RTP 43
Status: NP: RARE PASSAGE MIGRANT. Only 3 records, October (21st) to November (8th). Out Is: recorded only from Gd. Bahama (spring dates: 9, 11 April; extreme autumn dates: 13 August, 23 November), but no doubt occurs occasionally on most islands on migration.
Description: L 5½″ s A. This is a *brown-backed* swallow, distinguished from the similar Bank Swallow by its *dingy grey throat* and upper breast; the remaining underparts are pure white. An occasional Rough-winged Swallow is found among migrating Barn Swallows, but this is the rarest of the family.

BARN SWALLOW *Hirundo rustica* (English name: Swallow)   RTP 43
Status: NP: FAIRLY COMMON PASSAGE MIGRANT. There is a rather small spring passage in April and May, and a more important autumn one from August to November. Extreme dates: 7 April, 4 June*; 1 August, 1 December. Out Is: found throughout the Bahamas on migration. Extreme spring dates: Bimini, 28 March, 9 June. Late autumn date: San Salvador, 'end of December'.
Description, habits: L 7″ s A. The Barn Swallow has dark-blue upperparts, a *red throat*, and underparts that vary from pinkish to whitish according

to age. A good field-mark is the *deeply forked tail*, a true 'swallow-tail'. Barn Swallows feed with graceful, swooping flight over the ground or water, congregating wherever insects are abundant. They rest on telephone wires or reeds or, on the golf courses, on the ground. They are usually found in parties of 4 or 5, but flocks of 20, 30, or 50 birds are sometimes seen, often mixed with related species.

CLIFF SWALLOW *Petrochelidon pyrrhonota*   RTP 43
Status: NP: RARE PASSAGE MIGRANT. April (11th); August (30th) to October (12th). Out Is: recorded only from Gd. Bahama, but no doubt occurs on most islands on migration.
Description: L 6″ S A. This rare swallow is coloured like a Barn Swallow, with blue upperparts, white underparts, and a red face. It differs in having a short, *square* tail and a *pinkish rump*; no other swallow has a contrasting rump. I have mostly recorded poorly plumaged birds, presumably immatures, whose blue and red feathers were more often guessed at than seen, but there was no mistaking their pale rumps. This species is usually found in mixed flocks with other swallows.

PURPLE MARTIN *Progne subis*   RTP 43
Status: NP: UNCOMMON AUTUMN AND RARE SPRING MIGRANT. February (21st) to May (7th); September (2nd*) to October (4th). Out Is: presumably found sparingly throughout the Bahamas on migration. Extreme autumn dates: Gd. Bahama, 11 August, 15 October.
Description, habits: L 8″ A *large*, *dark*, *heavily built swallow*. The male has uniform dark-purple plumage, appearing black, and can hardly be confused with other swallows, all of which have more or less white underparts. The female has grey underparts, fading to whitish on the belly. Martins are distinctly uncommon, mostly appearing in September in ones and twos (and once, 12), sometimes with other swallows. They seem to fly higher than their relatives.

NUTHATCHES
Sittidae

BROWN-HEADED NUTHATCH *Sitta pusilla*   Pl 13; RTP 44
Status: NP: not found. Out Is: found only on Gd. Bahama, where it is resident in the pine barrens.

Description: L 4½″ s A. Known by its *brown cap* which extends down to the level of the eyes, and by the white spot on the nape. The upperparts are otherwise grey, the underparts whitish. Nuthatches creep about on tree-trunks and branches with an agility peculiar to their family.

MOCKINGBIRDS and THRASHERS
Mimidae

NORTHERN MOCKINGBIRD *Mimus polyglottos* (Local name: Thrasher) **Pl 8; RTP 46**

Status: NP: ABUNDANT RESIDENT. Out Is: resident on all main islands, except San Salvador and perhaps Crooked Is, but often less common than on New Providence.

Description, habits: L 10″ s A. The noisy and aggressive mockingbird is identified by its medium size, *grey plumage*, and long, expressive tail. In flight it shows *white patches on the wings* and on the sides of the tail. Almost every garden contains a pair of these familiar and conspicuous birds.

Though introduced on New Providence only 60 or 70 years ago, the Northern Mockingbird far outnumbers the native Bahama Mockingbird. This proliferation has no doubt been partly at the expense of the native species, but the two are to some extent non-competitive—the Northern prospering in the vicinity of houses and cultivated land, the Bahama in the wilder, rural areas.

Voice: the loud and musical song is usually delivered from a high perch, whether a tree, telephone wire, rooftop, or aerial. Individual singers vary enormously and the song itself is variable, but it is characterised by the repetition of each phrase three times. Occasionally heard at night. See Song Chart, p. 132. Among the birds most often imitated by the 'mocker' are the Grey Kingbird, Red-legged Thrush, Black-whiskered Vireo, Red-winged Blackbird, Mangrove Cuckoo, Bobwhite, Hairy Woodpecker, Yellowlegs, and Gull-billed Tern, but there is no limit to its talents as a mimic. The alarm note is a loud 'chek', and there is a grating note of anger. Young birds repeat a loud, monotonous 'dzeep, dzeep'.

Nest: loosely constructed of twigs, sparsely lined with grasses, placed from 2 to 25 feet up in a tree or bush, usually the latter. The 2 to 4 eggs are pale-greenish-blue, with reddish-brown markings zoned at the thick end. Building starts in February and March, eggs are laid in March, April, May, and June, the season ending in July.

BAHAMA MOCKINGBIRD *Mimus gundlachii*   Pl 10

Status: NP: FAIRLY COMMON RESIDENT. Out Is: resident throughout the Bahamas with the apparent exception of Gt. Abaco. Often abundant.

Description, habits: L 11″ s A. Similar to the preceding species, but larger, *browner*, and less often seen on New Providence. Distinguished in flight by the lack of white on the wings, and by the *white-tipped tail* (as compared with the white-*edged* tail of the commoner species). The Bahama Mockingbird also has more or less distinct stripes along the flanks and a broader tail—almost fan-shaped in flight. This is the native mockingbird of the Bahamas, but it is the scarcer of the two species on New Providence. One may infer that the Northern is slowly driving it out, but the pressure of human population (from 20 to 450 times denser on New Providence than on the out islands) is probably a factor of equal importance. Also, New Providence was, until a few hundred years ago, a pine-covered island, and the Bahama Mockingbird avoids such islands, as its distribution shows; probably it was never abundant here.

When it comes to actual fighting, the larger Bahama bird will put the Northern to flight every time—as I have repeatedly witnessed—but the sheer persistence of the smaller birds usually results in their occupying a disputed territory in the end. On New Providence, Bahama Mockingbirds are mostly found in dense, jungly coppice, spreading to more varied habitat out of the breeding season. On the out islands, they frequent coppice and scrub of all sorts, including very arid places and small cays. The habits of the Bahama Mockingbird do not greatly differ from those of its relative. It commonly feeds on insects on the ground and also takes berries and fruit, and I have seen one take a lizard. It is rather shyer than the other species, but on out islands will be found singing from prominent sprigs and on the telephone poles, often in remarkable numbers.

Voice: the song is loud and varied, and to my ears is more melodious and less strident than that of the preceding species. Certain characteristic notes (chéewee, chípwee, chípwoo, chéewoo) recur often enough to allow sure identification even if the singer is not seen. The song is delivered from a prominent perch, and the singer sometimes flutters a foot or two in the air and then falls back to its perch, a habit it shares with the Northern. The Bahama bird is not known to imitate the song of other species. The soft subsong is often heard in winter. There are various notes of anger or alarm: an explosive 'tchéeeoop', a strong 'chup', and a throaty, cuckoo-like 'cher, cher, cher' or 'chicker chuk chuk'.

Nest: similar to that of the preceding species. The eggs (2?) are stated to be whitish with spots. Brother Ignatius Dean cites an instance of the two species of mockingbird interbreeding.

PEARLY-EYED THRASHER *Margarops fuscatus*   **Pl 10**

Status: NP: not found. Out Is: resident in the southern Bahamas; found on most (perhaps all) islands from Eleuthera to Inagua. Thought to be spreading northwards.

Description: L 11″ s A. The *pale eyes and bill* distinguish this songbird from mockingbirds or thrushes, which it otherwise somewhat resembles. The plumage is brown, paler and striated on the underparts.

GRAY CATBIRD *Dumetella carolinensis* (Local name: Blue Thrasher)

RTP 46

Status: NP: COMMON WINTER VISITOR. Arrives in mid-October, becoming common by the end of the month; leaves during April and the first days of May. Extreme dates: 5 October*, 16 May. Out Is: found throughout the Bahamas in winter.

Description, habits: L 9″ s A. The Catbird is related to the mockingbirds and is of similar build. Its plumage is uniform *slate-grey*, with a *black cap* and rufous under tail-coverts; it is unmistakable if well seen. It usually frequents thick cover—coppice, scrub, tangled undergrowth, garden shrubbery, etc.—where it is easily overlooked in spite of its tameness.

Voice: the note from which it gets its name is a loud, cat-like wail. This is uttered constantly, sometimes by several birds together. It also makes a low 'quuck' (of concern?) and high, spitting notes (of alarm?). Although full song is not heard on New Providence, Catbirds often break into subsong, which is varied and melodious but only audible over a short distance. I have heard this in every month from October to April.

THRUSHES
Turdidae

RED-LEGGED THRUSH *Mimocichla plumbea* (Formerly Bahama Thrush)   **Pl 10**

Status: NP: COMMON RESIDENT. Out Is: found only in the northern half of the Bahamas (to Exuma Cays and Cat Is), and on Gt. Inagua.

Description, habits: L 10½″ s A. This large and handsome thrush is the only member of its family commonly found in the Bahamas. The plumage is *slate-grey*, which shows to advantage against the *bright-red legs and* *eye-ring*. The throat is black, with a white area near the bill, and the outer tail-feathers are tipped with white, very noticeable in flight. The feathers of the closed wing are edged with white.

The Red-legged Thrush inhabits wooded country: pine woods, casuarinas, coppice, thick undergrowth, and large gardens. It lives on the leaf-strewn woodland floor and obtains most of its food by foraging for insects under the dead leaves; in this way it makes loud, rustling sounds which often draw one's attention to a bird one might otherwise have missed. Apart from insects, it eats fruit and berries, and I have seen small frogs and lizards being carried to the nest. When disturbed, it usually flies a short distance to a low branch, and sometimes merely runs and hops away, showing little fear of human beings. Though normally a retiring bird, the Red-legged Thrush becomes noisy and aggressive in the breeding season: fights between three birds (presumably a pair and an intruding male) are common, and loud 'week-weekings' are heard on all sides. It is one of the last birds to go to roost, feeding well on into the dusk, and it is very noisy before finally settling down for the night.

Voice: the song is halting and melancholy, usually composed of two or three phrases which are repeated in varying order. Each phrase is separate from the next, like a sentence full of full stops: 'Chirri. Chirri. Eeyu. Chirri. Biyuyu.', etc. An exposed perch is usually chosen for singing, often high in a dead tree. See Song Chart, p. 132. Subsong is occasionally heard in the winter and spring. A weak, sibilant 'slee' is often uttered from low cover, and this note may be interspersed in the song at the beginning of the song period. The alarm-note is a loud, characteristic 'week week', sometimes repeated in crescendo. A quiet 'wuk wuk' expresses mild alarm. Young birds beg with an insistent 'chee, chee, chee'.

Nest: such nests as I have seen were placed 20 or 30 ft up in casuarinas at points where the trunks forked into separate branches, or in the 'eaves' of a palm tree, or on a low, rotted stump. Brother Ignatius Dean found a nest on the ground. The bulky and untidy nests were of grasses, casuarina needles, and bits of paper, on a foundation of leaves. The 3 or 4 eggs are pale-greenish-blue, heavily speckled with reddish-brown. The breeding season is from May until August.

SWAINSON'S THRUSH *Hylocichla ustulata* (Other name: Olive-backed Thrush)   RTP 45

Status: NP: RARE PASSAGE MIGRANT. Only 3 records: September (22nd) to October (28th*). Out Is: only recorded from Gd. Bahama, but is to be expected occasionally on most islands on migration.

Description: L 7″ s A. This dull-plumaged thrush has olive-brown upper-parts and pale underparts with dark spots on the upper breast. It closely resembles the next species, but is distinguished by its warm, buff-coloured cheeks and *distinct, buff eyering*.

GREY-CHEEKED THRUSH *Hylocichla minima* RTP 45
Status: NP: RARE PASSAGE MIGRANT. April (30th*) to May (13th*); October (3rd*–27th*). Out Is: almost no data, but no doubt occurs on most islands on migration.
Description: L 7″ s A. This seems to be the commonest of the North American thrushes that occur in the Bahamas; even so it is definitely rare. It is also the plainest of the thrushes, and is best identified by its *lack of conspicuous* markings. The Veery and the Hermit and Wood Thrushes (see Appendix) have partly reddish plumage, and the Swainson's has a pale eyering and a buff 'wash' on the cheeks and breast, but all of these field-marks are lacking on the Grey-cheeked, which is simply a duller, greyer version of the preceding species.

GNATCATCHERS
Sylviidae

BLUE-GREY GNATCATCHER *Polioptila caerulea* Pl 13; RTP 44
Status: NP: formerly resident, but now only an UNCOMMON AUTUMN PASSAGE MIGRANT. Seen regularly in September, October, and November, and single records from August (28th), December, and January (2nd). Out Is: recorded, and probably resident, on most main islands, though apparently absent from the central Bahamas. Common on some islands (e.g. Gt. Inagua).
Description, habits: L 4½″ s A. The tiny Gnatcatcher is known by its blue-grey upperparts, whitish underparts, and *long, white-bordered tail*. The general shape and pattern are reminiscent of a mockingbird; the size is that of a small warbler. The white eyering is noticeable at close quarters. A tame and very active bird, frequenting woodland and undergrowth. Records from New Providence are of special interest in view of the changed status of this species. A few pairs may reside, unobserved, in the pine

barrens, but I feel this to be unlikely as their call note would draw attention to them.

Voice: a thin, cross 'zpee zpi', 'zpeee zpizpeee', very distinctive.

STARLINGS
Sturnidae

STARLING *Sturnus vulgaris*   RTP 53

Status: NP: an UNCOMMON WINTER VISITOR at present (1962/63), but may be expected in increasing numbers. October (17th) to March (13th). Out Is: so far only recorded from the northern Bahamas (to San Salvador), but is spreading southwards.

Description, habits: L 8½″ S A. The Starling looks *uniformly black* at a distance, and its *pointed bill* and *short tail* give it a distinctive shape. At closer quarters a metallic purple and green gloss may be visible, and the plumage will be seen to be extensively spotted with white. In spring the beak changes from dusky to yellow. The flight is fast and direct. Gregarious. Starlings are fond of feeding on the ground, where they walk with waddling gait (most birds hop), but they are equally at home in the tops of royal palm trees or sallying out after insects, like a kingbird.

The aggressive Starling was first successfully introduced in the New World at New York in 1890, but since then it has multiplied and extended its range over most of North America. First recorded in the Bahamas in 1956, it is now appearing in increasing numbers: I noted 4 one winter (one was recorded the year before), 8 the next and 40 the next, but the following year, though a flock of 50 passed through, none remained for the winter. During part of the winter of 1962/63, however, more than 100 birds were present. Found in Nassau, in open country, in mangroves (with Red-winged Blackbirds), and in coppice.

Voice: the call is a loud whistle. The song consists of a jumbled-up medley of notes, and is heard from wintering birds.

VIREOS
Vireonidae

THICK-BILLED VIREO *Vireo crassirostris*   Pl 11

Status: NP: ABUNDANT RESIDENT. Out Is: common resident on all main islands.

Description, habits: L 5¼″ s A. During most of the year this species is most easily *identified by its song* (see 'Voice'). The upperparts are brownish-green, and the underparts pale yellowish, shading gradually to white (not in the clear-cut manner of the two following species). There are two whitish wing-bars, and the eyes are circled with yellow rings which meet above the beak, in the manner of spectacles. The plumage is usually clean and bright from November to June, but often 'moth-eaten' in the other months, when adults are moulting and many juveniles are about.

Though abundant, Thick-billed Vireos are easily overlooked for they frequent thickets and dense, jungly growth, where neither their deliberate movements nor their sober plumage attract attention. They are found in gardens, woods, and sometimes mangroves, but are commonest in thick coppice and scrub. They keep close together in pairs, never, except casually, being found with other species. Most of their feeding (insects, and an occasional berry) is done between 2 and 12 feet up, and they thus divide the food supply very evenly with our other common vireo, the Black-whiskered, which feeds among the higher foliage. The Thick-billed Vireo is very tame and is one of the easiest species to 'call' or 'whistle up', coming to within an arm's length without hesitation.

Voice: in contrast to its unassuming habits, this species is a loud, bold, and constant singer. The abrupt, emphatic song has ten or twelve variations, each one similar to the next, such as: 'chip chip WEEEoo chip', 'chip chip WEEE, chip yu', 'weecher chewistu cheewoo cher', 'chip chup WEEoo, chip chup weet', 'chip PEEEjawa, weechup'. No special perch is used for singing, the song being given while the bird moves about, feeding. In late summer the quieter, more sustained subsong may be heard. See Song Chart, p. 132. The alarm note is a rasping 'waaa, waaa, waaa', and a soft, conversational note is often heard between birds of a pair.

Nest: builds an insubstantial but beautiful cup-shaped nest of grasses, covered outside with moss and pieces of bark and, sometimes, bits of paper or rag. This is slung from a low branch (often the lowest branch of a casuarina) from 2 to 12 ft. up, but most often at a height of 3 or 4 ft. 2, occasionally 3, eggs are laid: white or very pale pink, thinly marked with blackish or reddish spots. The breeding season is short, most eggs being laid in April.

WHITE-EYED VIREO *Vireo griseus*   RTP 47
Status: NP: UNCOMMON WINTER VISITOR. October (4th*) to March (28th*). Out Is: recorded in winter from most main islands in the northern

Plate 11

Inagua Race

Plate 12

1. **Emerald Hummingbird**   page 75
   Male: bright green underparts.
   Female: greenish plumage; no rufous on underparts;
   forked tail.
   Andros, Gd. Bahama & Abaco.

2. **Bahama Woodstar**   75
   Male: violet throat; rufous underparts.
   Female: rufous underparts; rounded tail.
   Inagua race: violet throat *and* forehead.
   All islands.

3. **Bananaquit**   100
   Black white, and yellow plumage. Single white eye-stripe.
   Common, gardens.

4. **Bahama Yellowthroat**   114
   Male: black mask; yellow underparts.
   Female: plain, yellow underparts.
   Distinguished from Common Yellowthroat by absence
   of white on belly, yellowish upper border to mask,
   and slightly larger size and heavier bill.

5. **Olive-capped Warbler**   107
   Grey back; yellow throat; black streaks on flanks.

6. **Stripe-headed Tanager**   118
   Male: black, white, yellow and chestnut plumage.
   Two white head-stripes.
   Female: nondescript. White markings on wings.

7. **Black-faced Grassquit**   123
   Male: black underparts.
   Female: nondescript.
   Common, all islands.

8. **Yellow-faced Grassquit**   122
   Male: yellow stripe over eye and square throat-patch.
   Female: trace of same pattern as male.
   New Providence only.

9. **Melodious Grassquit**   124
   Black face; horseshoe-shaped yellow collar. New Providence only.

10. **Greater Antillean Bullfinch**   121
    Adult: black plumage; red patches.
    Immature: heavy bill; trace of red patches.

Bahamas, and from San Salvador. To be expected occasionally farther south. Late date: Andros, 4 April.

Description, habits: L 5″ s A. Though very similar to the preceding species, this is a *more brightly coloured* bird: its yellow 'spectacles' stand out against the greyish and white surrounding plumage, and its *yellow flanks* contrast with the white belly. The whitish eyes are noticeable at close quarters. The White-eyed Vireo is a more active bird than the preceding species and gives the impression of being smaller, though this may be chiefly due to its smarter plumage and less sluggish habits. Inhabits coppice, scrub, undergrowth, etc.

Voice: the song, heard in January and February, is very similar to that of the Thick-billed Vireo, but is just sufficiently different to attract attention, particularly on account of its greater speed and less emphatic delivery. There is a distinctive, churring alarm-note.

YELLOW-THROATED VIREO *Vireo flavifrons*   RTP 47, 51

Status: NP: UNCOMMON WINTER VISITOR. September (2nd) to April (14th). Seldom seen after mid-March. Out Is: very little data, but no doubt occurs in winter on at least the northern islands.

Description, habits: L 6″ s A. Distinguished from the Thick-billed Vireo by its bright *yellow throat and breast.* Otherwise the two birds are rather similar, with double white wingbars and yellow 'spectacles'. The colours of the Yellow-throated are brighter and the yellow breast terminates abruptly, the remaining underparts being pure white. The Yellow-throated Vireo is usually found among the middle or higher branches of trees, or in high coppice. Although more active than the Thick-billed, it is not easily noticed and in fact is rather elusive for such a brightly coloured bird.

Voice: the call is a distinctive, scolding 'chi-chi-chur-chur-chur-chur-chur'. The song, sometimes heard in February and March, is a succession of double-noted calls with a pause between each one: 'cheewee, cheewoo, uwee, cheewee', etc.

BLACK-WHISKERED VIREO *Vireo altiloquus*   Pl 11; RTP 60

Status: NP: COMMON SUMMER VISITOR. Arrives at the end of April, immediately making its presence known by its song. The departure in autumn, less easy to note as the birds are silent, takes place at the beginning of October. Extreme dates: 12 April, 21 October. Out Is: common in summer throughout the Bahamas.

Description, habits: L 6½″ s A. This vireo is best *identified by its song* (see

'Voice'). The plumage is olive-green on the upperparts and whitish on the underparts, with a greyish crown, a pale stripe above the eye, and a dark 'whisker' below the eye. See following species.

Black-whiskered Vireos frequent wooded country of all sorts, including coppice, high undergrowth, and gardens, and are found in sylvan parts of Nassau. They are birds of the higher foliage and move about unobtrusively in the treetops, being quite hard to locate when they are silent. They search with rather deliberate movements for their food (insects, and an occasional berry), sometimes hovering to take an otherwise inaccessible insect but generally not emerging from their leafy heights. The flight is strong but undulating.

Voice: the song, heard incessantly all through the day in early summer, is composed of short and almost identical phrases, with a pause of a second or two between each one: 'chip chewip; chip chewy; chi chur chewip; chip chewip' and so on. See Song Chart, p. 132. The call or alarm note is a drawling 'mweee' or 'yeeea'. Young birds beg with a squeaky 'treep'.

Nest: similar to that of the Thick-billed Vireo, but usually at a higher elevation. Stated to lay 2 or 3 pinkish and heavily spotted eggs, but I think that frequently only one young bird is raised. Laying seems to take place in late May and young birds are seen out of the nest from July onwards.

RED-EYED VIREO *Vireo olivaceus* RTP 47

Status: NP: UNCOMMON PASSAGE MIGRANT. September (16th) to November (3rd), most records being for October. No recent spring records. Out Is: Presumably found sparingly throughout the Bahamas on migration. Late date: Gd. Bahama, 13 November.

Description, habits: L 6″ s A. Essentially similar to the preceding species, the Red-eyed is presumably the parent stock and the Whiskered an offshoot formed over the centuries by Caribbean Red-eyes. The only reliable difference that is noticeable in the field is the *whisker mark* of the local birds, *lacking* on the present species.

Red-eyed Vireos arrive just when the Whiskereds are leaving, and the two species are found together for only a few weeks (late September, early October). The probability is that a vireo of this type seen before mid-September is a Whiskered and seen after mid-October is a Red-eyed. I have not noticed any difference between the habits of the two species, and their choice of habitat is identical, the Red-eyeds being found in the very same trees that the Whiskereds frequent.

Voice: similar to that of the Black-whiskered Vireo, but the present species is usually silent on New Providence.

HONEYCREEPERS
Coerebidae

BANANAQUIT *Coereba flaveola* (Formerly Bahama Bananaquit, Bahama Honeycreeper. Local name: Banana Bird)   Pl 12; RTP 60
Status: NP: ABUNDANT RESIDENT. Out Is: common resident on all islands.
Description, habits: L 5″ s A. An attractive and popular garden bird. The upperparts are *black* with a white line above the eye, the underparts *white*, with a broad *yellow sash* across the breast. The slightly curved bill is distinctive at close quarters, and in flight the yellow rump is noticeable. Two individuals in my garden had a black sash below the yellow one; melanism in Bananaquits is quite common. Immatures, which are seen almost all year round, have grey upperparts, whitish underparts, and little or no yellow on the breast. The 'banana bird' is commonest in and around gardens, but also frequents scrub, undergrowth, open woodlands, etc. It feeds mainly on the nectar of flowers and the small insects it finds in the nectar, but it is also fond of fruit and berries. Unable to hover in front of flowers as hummingbirds do, the Bananaquit resorts to all sorts of entertaining acrobatics to obtain the nectar, hanging upside-down or clinging unsteadily to a swaying stem. While they cannot be said to flock, they are sociable birds, and many are found together where flowers or fruit are abundant. We ringed 17 in our garden in two days and still left many unringed. They are either playful or pugnacious or both, for they constantly attack and chase one another. Some of these chases have a sexual significance but others seem to denote nothing more than an overwhelming *joie de vivre*. The flight is fast and direct, a whirring sound being audible from close by.
Voice: the true song of the Bananaquit is a sweet trilling, increasing in speed towards the end. Both before and after the song it commonly makes various unmusical 'bubbling' and 'reeling' sounds, and indeed its attempts at song during the second half of the year consist almost entirely of these sounds, heard from both adults and immatures. The song is delivered either while perched or in flight, frequently both. See Song Chart, p. 132. The call-note is a loud 'quit', the note of alarm a softer 'chip'. Young birds call monotonously: 'chit, chit, chit', sounding rather like warblers.
Nest: builds a rounded nest of grasses and fibres, with the entrance in the lower half, facing downwards. The nests are usually placed in vertical forks of bushes, saplings, or trees, from 5 to 50 ft, but generally between

7 and 10 ft, from the ground. Strange sites are sometimes chosen, e.g. in a lamp on a porch, where the sitting bird would surely have been roasted if the light had been turned on. Often builds several nests in quick succession to no apparent purpose, sometimes leaving them half-finished. Adults are known to roost in nests all year round. Although it is stated that 3 eggs are normally laid (and clutches of 4 have been recorded), I have usually found only 2. They are slightly elongated and are white, speckled with red-brown and zoned round the thick end. Breeding takes place during almost the whole year, though the main season is from February to April.

WARBLERS (WOOD WARBLERS)
Parulidae

This huge family (33 species in the main text, 8 in the Appendix) contains many of our common species. Their plumages are varied and often beautiful, but sometimes confusing. My brief written descriptions will often prove inadequate, and anyone who really wishes to master this family should study the coloured illustrations in Peterson's *Field Guide to the Birds*. A beginner should in any case start by identifying the commoner species, which are, in approximate order of commonness: Palm Warbler (by far the most abundant of the family), Prairie Warbler, American Redstart, Common Yellowthroat, Northern Waterthrush, Ovenbird, Yellow-throated Warbler, and Black-and-White Warbler. He should then progress to the less common but still quite numerous species, which are: Cape May, Northern Parula, Magnolia, Yellow-rumped, Black-throated Blue, Blackpoll, and Worm-eating Warblers, and Louisiana Waterthrush.

Warblers are small, active, mainly insect-eating birds, most of which range widely among trees and bushes and often into gardens (we saw 29 species in ours). Almost all of them have a 'chipping' call note, a fact that I have purposely omitted from the individual texts. It should be noted that with two, possibly three, exceptions, all the warblers are winter visitors and/or passage migrants on New Providence.

BLACK-AND-WHITE WARBLER *Mniotilta varia*   RTP 49
Status: NP: COMMON WINTER VISITOR. First arrives during August, and becomes common in September. Leaves in April. Extreme dates: 31 July*, 8 May. Out Is: found throughout the Bahamas in winter.
Description, habits: L 5¼" Little remains to be added to the description '*black and white*', the plumage being striped black and white above, white

beneath. The male has a black throat, lacking on the female, and immature birds show a brownish wash on the flanks and underparts. The habits of this species are different from those of most other warblers as it obtains most of its insect food from crevices in the bark of trees and in consequence is an *expert tree-creeper*, working the branches and tree-trunks with great agility. Frequents wooded country of all sorts.

Voice: sometimes sings in October, November, and April: a pleasant, soft 'teesa weesa weesa weesa wee'.

PROTHONOTARY WARBLER *Protonotaria citrea*   RTP 50, 52
Status: NP: UNCOMMON PASSAGE MIGRANT. April (2nd–23rd); August (6th) to October (12th). Out Is: only recorded from the northern islands, but no doubt occurs sparingly throughout the Bahamas on migration. Late autumn date: Harbour Is, 27 November.

Description: L 5½″ Known by its *bright golden head* and underparts, which contrast with the dark upperparts and *blue-grey wings*. Females are duller than males, and the dark colouring of the back extends on to the nape and head. Although stated to inhabit swamp-lands in the breeding season, the Prothonotary Warbler occurs in various types of habitat on migration, usually on or near the ground.

WORM-EATING WARBLER *Helmitheros vermivorus*   RTP 48
Status: NP: FAIRLY COMMON WINTER VISITOR. Arrives during September and leaves during April. Extreme dates: 31 August*, 1 May. Out Is: probably occurs throughout the Bahamas in winter, though not recorded from all islands. Early date: Bimini, 18 August.

Description, habits: L 5¼″ s A. Easily recognised by its sober *olive and buff* plumage and *black-striped head*; it has stripes through the eyes and two on the crown. This unobtrusive warbler is stated to feed mostly on the ground in summer, but in its winter quarters—on New Providence at least—it is almost entirely arboreal. It is particularly fond of searching dead leaves hanging among bushes and trees, so making loud rustling sounds that have drawn my attention to it countless times.

BLUE-WINGED WARBLER *Vermivora pinus*   RTP 50
Status: NP: RARE PASSAGE MIGRANT. February (28th) to April (12th); September (17th) to October (2nd*). Out Is: seldom recorded, but no doubt occurs on passage throughout the Bahamas. Reported as late as 1 January (San Salvador), so may occasionally remain in winter.

Description: L 4¾″ s A. Known by its *bright-yellow* forehead and under-parts and by the *black line* running back from the bill through the eye. The upperparts are greenish, and the wings grey with two white wingbars.

TENNESSEE WARBLER *Vermivora peregrina*   RTP 48, 52
Status: NP: UNCOMMON PASSAGE MIGRANT. October (5th* to 28th). Out Is: no doubt found on all islands on autumn migration. Spring date: Bimini, 7 April. Late autumn date: Andros, 25 November.
Description: L 4¾″ s A. A plain, inconspicuous warbler, with uniformly green upperparts and pale-yellow underparts. A light stripe over the eye, a faint, dark line through the eye, and the *white under tail-coverts* are the only field-marks. Not recommended for beginners. This is one of the rarer warblers, but small parties (up to 6 birds) are sometimes found together.

NASHVILLE WARBLER *Vermivora ruficapilla*   RTP 50, 52
Status: NP: RARE PASSAGE MIGRANT. September (30th) to October (25th). Out Is: recorded from Gd. Bahama, Harbour Is.: (24 November), and Eleuthera (mid-February). No doubt occurs sparingly on migration on most islands.
Description: L 4¾″ s A. Identified by its *greyish head*, greenish back, *yellow throat* and underparts, and white eyering. Its yellow throat distinguishes it from the rather similar Connecticut and Mourning Warblers.

NORTHERN PARULA WARBLER *Parula americana*   RTP 48, 56
Status: NP: FAIRLY COMMON WINTER VISITOR. Arrives chiefly in October, and leaves in April and the first days of May. Extreme dates: 21 August, 13 May. Out Is: found throughout the Bahamas in winter.
Description, habits: L 4½″ These attractive little warblers have *bluish* upperparts with white wingbars, and mostly yellow underparts. The posterior underparts are white (Magnolia Warbler, yellow). There is a *greenish patch* on the back, a valuable field-mark, and males have a dark, chestnut band across the breast. Winter and immature birds have duller, greener upperparts. See Prairie and Magnolia Warblers. The Parula is a typical arboreal warbler; it searches the trees and bushes with active movements, often hovering to pick an insect off the underside of a leaf.
Voice: The trilling song is occasionally heard in April and May.

YELLOW WARBLER *Dendroica petechia*   **Pl 13; RTP 50, 51**
Status: NP: FAIRLY COMMON RESIDENT (in spite of reports to the contrary). Out Is: found throughout the islands, being the only resident warbler in the southern half of the Bahamas.
Description, habits: L 5½" Known, as its name suggests, by its yellow plumage: lemon-yellow on the underparts, greenish-yellow on the upperparts. Males have reddish streakings on the breast. A great many warblers have partly yellow plumage, but none give such an *all-yellow appearance* in the field. Other points to note are *the song*, its liking for *mangroves*, and its presence in summer, particularly in the warblerless months of June and July.

Yellow Warblers tend to keep out of sight, moving unobtrusively among the mangroves, and one's attention might never be drawn to them were it not for their song. They seem to prefer coastal mangroves, and are numerous along the south coast (e.g. Coral Harbour, South Beach), but do not frequent apparently suitable inland localities. They are sometimes found away from mangroves in August and September, and again in winter and spring—when I have even recorded them in my garden—but these are probably North American migrants.
Voice: the song is a distinctive, pleasing 'tsee tsee tsee tsee titiwee', heard from March to September.
Nest: stated to be a small cup, presumably placed in mangroves, with 2–3 eggs. Adults seen carrying food in May; young seen out of the nest in July.

MAGNOLIA WARBLER *Dendroica magnolia*   **RTP 49, 51**
Status: NP: FAIRLY COMMON WINTER VISITOR. Arrives in October and leaves at the end of April and in early May. Is commoner on passage, notably in October, than in winter. Extreme dates: 20 September, 20 May. Out Is: no doubt occurs throughout the Bahamas on passage and in winter though, surprisingly, it is not recorded from all islands.
Description, habits: L 5" The Magnolia Warbler is best identified, in winter, by its *call-note* and by the broad, *white band* on its dark tail. The rest of the plumage is greenish on the upperparts and yellow on the underparts, with indistinct dark streaks along the flanks. See Prairie and Parula Warblers. In summer, the upperparts are dark-grey, with white wing- and tail-markings, and the yellow underparts are boldly striped with black, but this plumage is only seen in April and May. Magnolias behave much as other warblers, actively searching for insects among undergrowth

and woodland tangles and seldom staying still for more than a second or two.

Voice: the call is a distinctive, chirping 'tweep' or 'tzeep'.

CAPE MAY WARBLER *Dendroica tigrina*   RTP 49, 51

Status: NP: FAIRLY COMMON WINTER VISITOR. Arrives in September and leaves during April. Commoner as a migrant than during the winter, being particularly numerous in April. Extreme dates: 30 August, 13 May. Out Is: found throughout the Bahamas in winter.

Description, habits: L 5″ In full plumage, the upperparts are greenish and the rump and underparts *bright-yellow*, the latter *heavily streaked with black*. Males have bright chestnut patches on the cheeks. Females and immatures lack the yellow colouring in winter and are among the most difficult warblers to identify; they are brown-plumaged and are best told by their heavily streaked underparts and by the light patch on the side of the neck. Cape Mays are less active than many warblers and more strictly tree-dwelling. They are very fond of fruit and berries in addition to the usual warbler diet of insects, and when they locate a tree with ripe berries they become very pugnacious, fighting among themselves and ejecting other warblers.

Voice: I have heard the song only once (6 April), and noted it as 'chi-chi-chi-chi-chi-chi-chip', all on one note.

BLACK-THROATED BLUE WARBLER *Dendroica caerulescens*
                                                            RTP 48, 52

Status: NP: FAIRLY COMMON WINTER VISITOR. Arrives in late September and in October, and leaves in April and the first days of May. An influx of migrants is noticeable in April. Extreme dates: 17 September, 14 May. Out Is: no doubt occurs throughout the Bahamas in winter, though not recorded from all islands.

Description, habits: L 5¼″ The male is easily identified by its *dark-blue upperparts*, *black throat* and flanks, and white underparts. Females, on the other hand, have greenish upperparts and yellowish underparts and are very nondescript except for a small *white spot on the closed wing*, and even this is lacking on some birds. Then one must rely on the pale 'eyebrow' and the whitish ring under the eye. Black-throated Blue Warblers feed rather unobtrusively on the ground and low down in tangled undergrowth; insects are the main food but berries are also taken.

Voice: the call-note is a soft but incisive 'tchip' and the alarm a louder 'chick' or 'check', both notes being distinctive in quality. Occasionally heard singing in April, a throaty 'soo soo soo sweee' and 'seoo soo soo wee tweetwee'.

YELLOW-RUMPED WARBLER *Dendroica coronata* (Formerly Myrtle Warbler) RTP 49, 51

Status: NP: variable—usually an UNCOMMON WINTER VISITOR AND COMMON SPRING MIGRANT. Seldom at all numerous before December; sometimes common from then on, though most years they remain scarce until February, when the spring migration begins; this lasts until late April. Extreme dates: 18 September, 29 April. Also, exceptionally, 5 June. Out Is: occurs throughout the Bahamas in winter.

Description, habits: L 5¼″ Rather nondescript in winter plumage, with rich-brown upperparts, streaked with black, and pale, streaked underparts, tinged with yellow on the flanks. Distinguished from similar species (Palm Warbler, immature Cape May Warbler) by its *bright yellow rump*, most noticeable in flight. In breeding plumage there are yellow patches on the crown and shoulders, and dark markings on the head and breast. This plumage is seldom seen on New Providence, but the yellow crown-mark becomes quite distinct on some individuals from February onwards. It is difficult to assign any special habits or habitat to this species: it may be found low down over water, high in deciduous or pine trees, in coppice, or with Palm Warblers on a golf course. It is usually found in small groups, particularly in the spring.

BLACK-THROATED GREEN WARBLER *Dendroica virens* RTP 49, 51

Status: NP: UNCOMMON WINTER VISITOR. September (21st) to April (23rd). Out Is: very few records, but no doubt occurs sparingly throughout the Bahamas in winter.

Description, habits: L 5″ Known by its greenish upperparts, two white wingbars, white underparts, and *bright yellow cheeks*, In addition many birds have black throats, but this varies according to age, sex, and season, and may be lacking. This is a typical wood warbler, frequenting trees and shady tangles where it searches for insects with quick movements and brief, hovering flights.

BLACKBURNIAN WARBLER *Dendroica fusca* RTP 48, 51

Status: NP: RARE AUTUMN PASSAGE MIGRANT. August (19th) to September (30th*). Out Is: seldom recorded, but no doubt occurs on most islands on migration. Late date: Gd. Bahama, 14 November.

Description: L 5¼″ In autumn plumage, the general colour of the upperparts is brownish, relieved by two distinct wingbars and *pale stripes on the back*. There is a yellow line over the eye, the throat is yellow, and the remaining underparts are white with dark streaks along the flanks.

YELLOW-THROATED WARBLER *Dendroica dominica* Pl 13; RTP 49
Status: NP: COMMON WINTER VISITOR. The first winter visitor to arrive; first seen during July, becoming common in August. Leaves early in the spring, seldom remaining later than mid-March. Extreme dates: 15 July, 22 April*. Out Is: found throughout the Bahamas in winter, and a local race is resident in the pine woods of Gd. Bahama and Abaco.
Description, habits: L 5¼″ s A. Known by its grey upperparts and white underparts, set off by a bright *yellow throat and chest*. The horseshoe shape of this, together with the *black-and-white patterning of the face* and black streakings along the flanks make identification easy. No differences between male and female, adult and immature, nor winter and summer plumages. The Yellow-throated Warbler flies less, is less active and less sociable than most other warblers, seeking its insect food among the upper branches of trees, generally quite unobtrusively. Fond of pines, casuarinas, and palms, but by no means confined to these trees.

OLIVE-CAPPED WARBLER *Dendroica pityophila*   Pl 12
Status: NP: not found. Out Is: resident in the pine barrens of Gd. Bahama and Abaco only.
Description: L 5″ s A. A grey-backed and yellow-throated warbler, distinguished from the preceding species by the *lack* of black-and-white markings on the head and by its olive-green crown. Both species have black streakings along the flanks, extensive on the Yellow-throated Warbler, confined to a small area on the Olive-capped.

CHESTNUT-SIDED WARBLER *Dendroica pensylvanica*   RTP 49, 51
Status: NP: RARE PASSAGE MIGRANT. September (15th) to October (25th). No recent spring records. Out Is: not recorded, but no doubt occurs on migration.
Description: L 5″ Easily identified in spring by its yellow crown and chestnut flanks. Autumn birds have clear, yellowish-green upperparts, white underparts, two *yellow wingbars*, and white eyerings. This green and white pattern, in conjunction with the wingbars, is distinctive. Some autumn birds show *traces of chestnut* on the flanks, in which case they can only be

confused with the next species, which has a darker-green back, streaked with black.

BAY-BREASTED WARBLER *Dendroica castanea*   RTP 49, 51

Status: NP: RARE PASSAGE MIGRANT. October (4th*) to November (5th*). Out Is: recorded only from Gd. Bahama and Eleuthera (3 October, 6 November), but no doubt occurs occasionally on most islands.

Description: L 5″ In autumn plumage, resembles an autumn Blackpoll, with greenish upperparts, dark stripes on the back, two wingbars, and whitish underparts. The legs, however, are dark (pale on Blackpolls). Some birds still show traces of their summer plumage, notably *chestnut on the flanks*. See preceding species.

BLACKPOLL WARBLER *Dendroica striata*   RTP 49, 51

Status: NP: FAIRLY COMMON PASSAGE MIGRANT. The main passage is in May and October. Extreme dates: 8 April, 7 June; 16 September*, 12 November*. Out Is: found throughout the Bahamas on migration. Late autumn date: Harbour Is, 29 November.

Description, habits: L 5½″ The male is easily recognised in spring by its *black cap* and *white cheeks*. (The rather similar Black-and-white Warbler has a striped head.) Females in spring and both sexes in autumn are dingy, greenish-grey birds, but, when well seen, the combination of *pale legs*, white under tail-coverts, wingbars, and *striped back* distinguishes them. This is the only one of the commoner warblers that is exclusively a bird of passage in the Bahamas. The main spring passage takes place around 10 to 15 May, when most other warblers have left, but in autumn they come through with the seasonal rush of other birds and, with their dull plumage, are easily overlooked. Blackpolls feed quietly in coppice, undergrowth, and the lower branches of trees—particularly pines and casuarinas.

PINE WARBLER *Dendroica pinus*   Pl 13; RTP 49, 51

Status: NP: COMMON RESIDENT. Out Is: resident on the pine-forested northern islands: Andros, Gd. Bahama, and Abaco. Also recorded from Harbour Is and Cay Sal.

Description, habits: L 5¼″ The Pine Warbler is well named, for it is *found almost exclusively in pine trees*, notably in the barrens on the southern and western parts of the island. Adult males have olive upperparts with two white wingbars, a yellow throat and breast, and white belly. At close quarters the yellow plumage is seen to be indistinctly streaked. Females and immatures are duller, often with little or no yellow on the under-parts, and are sometimes difficult to identify. The easiest way to get to know this species is to go to the pine barrens in summer, *listen for the song*, and then look for the singer. In midsummer there are no other warblers in that habitat on New Providence. Pine Warblers often appear to be curious about human intruders, and will approach deliberately to within a few feet and even hover in front of one's face. Normally, however, they will be found feeding and flying about among well-grown pines, from ground level to the treetops.

Voice: the song is a loud, musical trill, which brightens the otherwise rather lifeless pine barrens. Heard from late February to November, but chiefly from April to July.

Nest: presumably placed on branches of pine trees. In North America 4 white eggs, spotted with brown, are laid. The nesting season seems to reach a peak in June, and many young are seen from July onwards.

KIRTLAND'S WARBLER *Dendroica kirtlandii*   RTP 49

Status: NP: apparently a RARE WINTER VISITOR. Out Is: a sprinkling of records, covering most islands. October to May (5th).

Description: L 5¾″ S A. This rare warbler has dark upperparts (grey in breeding plumage, brownish-grey in winter) and yellow underparts with dark streaks along the flanks. The back is streaked with black, and there are two faint wingbars and a broken eyering. The Kirtland's shares the Palm and Prairie Warblers' habit of wagging its tail constantly. The world population of Kirtland's Warblers is estimated at only 1,000 birds. They breed in Michigan and winter exclusively in the Bahamas, but 1,000 birds become extremely elusive when dispersed over 4,400 square miles of land.

PRAIRIE WARBLER *Dendroica discolor*   RTP 49, 51

Status: NP: ABUNDANT WINTER VISITOR. Arrives during August and is present in large numbers by the end of that month. Leaves principally during the second half of March, but some birds linger on until mid-April—a few (usually in immature plumage) being seen still later. Extreme dates: 20 July†, 13 May. Out Is: found throughout the Bahamas in winter.

Description, habits: L 4¾″ S A. In adult plumage the upperparts are greenish-brown and the whole underparts *bright lemon-yellow*, boldly striped with black along the flanks. Distinguished from similar species by its *black facial markings*, in particular an 'inverted eyebrow' *under* the eye. Wags its tail up and down. Immatures have duller plumage than adults, but the distinctive facial markings remain visible. The Prairie is a typical wood warbler; it feeds with agile movements among the foliage, seldom remaining still for more than a few seconds at a time. It is the commonest yellow-plumaged warbler.

Voice: the song, heard regularly in March and April (and once in September) is a soft, plaintive, ascending scale with a flourish at the end: 'weet weet weet weet weetitiweet'.

PALM WARBLER *Dendroica palmarum*   RTP 49, 51

Status: NP: ABUNDANT WINTER VISITOR. Arrives in October in large flocks which split up into ones, twos, and small parties during the course of the month. Leaves chiefly during the first half of April. Extreme dates: 19 September*, 17 May. Out Is: found throughout the Bahamas in winter.

Description, habits: L 5″ S A. The friendly and abundant Palm Warbler is best identified by its habit of feeding on the ground (flying to a tree or wall when alarmed) and the *constant wagging of its tail*. The winter plumage is brownish and nondescript, with a trace of yellow on the under tail-coverts. Some birds begin changing their plumage in February, and by March many of them have the bright yellow breasts and chestnut crowns of their breeding plumage. Palm Warblers are chiefly *remarkable for their abundance*; in winter one warbler in every two is a Palm, and bird-watching is a succession of false alarms until one has learnt to recognise them at a glance. They are widely distributed in open country and around houses; less common in woodland.

Voice: Brother Ignatius Dean tells me that he has heard the song in spring.

OVENBIRD *Seiurus aurocapillus*   RTP 48

Status: NP: COMMON WINTER VISITOR. Arrives in early October. Most local birds seem to leave again by the end of April, their place being taken by a noticeable wave of migrants which are found till mid-May. Extreme dates: 1 September, 24 May. Out Is: found throughout the Bahamas in winter. Early date: Gd. Bahama, 15 Aug.

Description, habits: L 6″ S A. This close relative of the waterthrushes has brown upperparts and white underparts, with black spots on the breast and flanks. It has a *white* eyering, which gives it a surprised expression, a dull *orange-coloured crown* bordered with black, and pale legs. The Ovenbird is found in coppice, deciduous woods, thick undergrowth, and shrubbery, walking with cocked tail and mincing steps over the fallen leaves among which it finds its food (insects; also berries; once a small lizard; fond of bread). Though tame and numerous, Ovenbirds are easily overlooked for they seldom leave thick cover and will allow one to walk past without showing much concern. On such occasions they may fly to a low branch, but otherwise they are always found on the ground.

Voice: the alarm note is a loud 'chip', louder and deeper than the chipping notes of other warblers. Sometimes repeated incessantly by a single bird or several together. I have occasionally heard the song—a ringing 'teacher teacher teacher teach'—at dawn in early May.

NORTHERN WATERTHRUSH *Seiurus noveboracensis*   RTP 48
Status: NP: COMMON WINTER VISITOR. Arrives in late August, becoming common in September. I think that the majority of local birds leave during April and that most of those seen in May are migrants. Extreme dates: 19 August, 28 May. Out Is: found throughout the Bahamas in winter. Early date: Gd. Bahama, 13 August.
Description, habits: L $5\frac{1}{2}''$ s A. This, the commoner of the two water-thrushes, looks like a small thrush, having brown upperparts, pale buffish underparts, and a buff stripe above the eye. The underparts are heavily striped. See following species. The Northern Waterthrush is usually found in the vicinity of water, whether pools, ponds, mangrove swamps and adjacent coast, or flooded undergrowth. It is also quite common in damp spots in woodland and gardens. Both this species and the next are usually seen on the ground, where they run actively to and fro, turning over sodden leaves or picking insects off the water. They share with the Spotted Sandpiper the habit of 'teetering', or moving the body up and down unceasingly.
Voice: the alarm note is a loud, distinctive 'pink', often repeated over and over and taken up by all the other waterthrushes within hearing. An occasional burst of song is heard (October, March) and one of a small belated group was in full song (28 May). This is a pleasing falling cadence: 'twit twit twit twee twee twee chew chew chew'.

LOUISIANA WATERTHRUSH *Seiurus motacilla*   RTP 48
Status: NP: FAIRLY COMMON WINTER VISITOR. Arrives a full month earlier and leaves again some two months earlier than the preceding species. First seen in the second half of July, reaching full strength in August. Becomes scarcer from January onwards, usually disappearing altogether by the end of March. Extreme dates: 17 July, 17 April. Out Is: little data available; presumably found throughout the Bahamas in winter.

Plate 13

1. **Pine Warbler** page 108
   Greenish above; yellowish below, faintly streaked. Wing
   bars. Pine woods. Absent southern islands.

2. **Yellow-throated Warbler** 107
   Yellow throat; black and white head pattern.

3. **Yellow Warbler** 104
   Yellow plumage; reddish streakings.
   Mangroves.

4. **Blue-grey Gnatcatcher** 93
   Blue-grey and whitish plumage. Eye-ring. Long tail.

5. **Brown-headed Nuthatch** 88
   Brown cap; white spot on nape.
   Grand Bahama only.

6. **Red-winged Blackbird** 117
   Black; scarlet shoulder patch.
   Absent southern islands.

Description, habits: L 6¼″ s A. Differences between this and the preceding species are slight but distinct. The Louisiana is a *brighter-plumaged* bird, with a broad, *white stripe over the eye*, and white underparts which contrast with a rufous tinge on the flanks and buffy under tail-coverts. These white, rufous, and buff areas are, on the Northern, all of one colour: buff. The Louisiana is slightly larger and seems to have more brightly coloured legs. It is less common than the preceding species. Louisiana Waterthrushes are usually found in the immediate neighbourhood of fresh or brackish water, often with Northerns. The Northern appears to tolerate drier conditions and saltier water, and so ranges more widely than the Louisiana. The general habits of the two waterthrushes are very similar.

Voice: 'pink', similar to the preceding species but slightly louder. The song, often heard in August and September and again, less frequently, in January and February, starts with 3 or 4 sweet, clear notes 'cheer, cheer, cheer' and then breaks into a jumble of descending notes of poorer quality.

KENTUCKY WARBLER *Oporornis formosus*   RTP 50
Status: NP: RARE PASSAGE MIGRANT. April (4th–15th); August (11th) to October (12th). Out Is: one record from Gd. Bahama. No doubt occurs sparingly on other islands on migration.
Description: L 5½″ Males have uniform olive upperparts and yellow underparts, and are identified by the broad, whisker-like, *black line down the cheeks*. The incomplete, yellow eyering and the black line from the bill to the eye are also noticeable. Females are similar, but less distinctly marked. Fond of feeding on or near the ground.

CONNECTICUT WARBLER *Oporornis agilis*   RTP 50, 52
Status: NP: RARE PASSAGE MIGRANT. May (9th*–10th*); September (23rd) to November (18th*). Out Is: seldom recorded, but to be expected on most islands on migration.
Description: L 5½″ Known by its dark upperparts, *dusky throat* and upper breast, yellowish underparts and white *eyering*. The similar Nashville Warbler has the entire underparts (throat included) yellow. Females and immatures have the throat and upper breast a less distinct, brownish colour, but the division between the dark throat and breast and yellowish belly is still visible, as is the eyering at all times.

COMMON YELLOWTHROAT *Geothlypis trichas*   RTP 50, 52

Status: NP: COMMON WINTER VISITOR. Arrives in October and leaves during April and in early May. Extreme dates: 3 September*, 24 May. Out Is: found throughout the Bahamas in winter.

Description, habits: L 5″ Males are identified by the *black mask* across their faces. They have dull brown upperparts and a yellow throat and breast, but the black mask precludes confusion with other yellow-breasted warblers except the following species. Females are rather nondescript but are known by their pale-yellow 'bib' and white belly. Yellowthroats are most abundant in mangrove swamps and damp or marshy places, but they also frequent long grass, gardens, woods, undergrowth, and coppice. They are seldom found higher than 2 or 3 ft. from the ground, usually skulking in thick vegetation and keeping out of sight. When flushed, their quick, jerky flight normally takes them only as far as the next patch of cover.

Voice: the usual note is a distinctive, throaty 'cherp'. Not heard singing.

BAHAMA YELLOWTHROAT *Geothlypis rostrata*   Pl 12

Status: NP: believed to be a RARE RESIDENT. Out Is: found on Andros, Gd. Bahama, Abaco, Eleuthera and Cat Is. Apparently common in places.

Description, habits: L 6″ Similar to the preceding species but *larger*, and males have the *whole underparts yellow*. The upper border of the mask is stated to be yellowish (bluish-white on the common species). The Bahama Yellowthroat has been seen or collected at different times of year at St Augustine's Monastery and on the ridge south of Lake Cunningham, and is thought to be resident. Personally I have not encountered this species, so can only contribute the observation that it must be of rare or irregular occurrence. It should be remembered that the preceding species—an infinitely commoner bird during nine months of the year—is normally absent during June, July, and August, so any yellowthroat seen during those months should be carefully observed, as should any yellowthroat seen singing, pairing, or, of course, nesting. Habitat: coppice and scrub.

Voice: the call-note is stated to be noticeably different from that of the Common Yellowthroat—'less harsh'. The song of both species is a distinctive 'wichitee wichitee wichitee wich'.

Nest: the only known nest, found by Collett on Eleuthera, was in a tree-stump and contained 2 young.

HOODED WARBLER *Wilsonia citrina*   RTP 50, 52

Status: NP: UNCOMMON PASSAGE MIGRANT, OCCASIONAL WINTER

VISITOR. September (3rd*) to April (28th). Most frequently recorded in October, when on passage, but a few remain all winter. Out Is: very little data, but no doubt occurs sparingly throughout the Bahamas.

Description, habits: L 5½″ Both sexes have uniform olive-green upperparts and yellow underparts, but the male is distinguished by the *black hood* which encircles the *bright-yellow face*. Females and immatures have no distinctive field-marks other than their yellow foreheads and white markings in the tail. Hooded Warblers are usually seen on the ground in some damp and shady place among undergrowth. They constantly flick their wings and tail (showing the white markings) and make short, fluttering rushes after insects.

Voice: the note is a high-pitched 'cheet', different from most warbler calls.

CANADA WARBLER *Wilsonia canadensis* RTP 49, 52

Status: NP: RARE AUTUMN PASSAGE MIGRANT. September (2nd) to October (12th). Out Is: not recorded, but no doubt occurs on migration.

Description: L 5½″ The Canada Warbler has plain, dark-grey upperparts, yellow underparts, vireo-like *yellow 'spectacles'* and pale legs. Best identified by the short, vertical black streaks on the upper breast, which form a sort of *'necklace'* (though this may be faint or lacking on females and immatures).

AMERICAN REDSTART *Setophaga ruticilla* RTP 48

Status: NP: ABUNDANT WINTER VISITOR. First arrives in August, becoming common in September. Leaves late in the spring, commonly remaining till mid-May. Extreme dates: 3 August, 28 May. Out Is: found throughout the Bahamas in winter. There is an unusual summer record, 4 July, from Cat Is, and a June record from Andros.

Description, habits: L 5″ Adult males are unmistakable, with *jet-black* head and upperparts, white underparts, and *flame-red markings on the wings and tail*. Females and immatures, which far outnumber adult males, have greyish-green upperparts and *pale yellow* markings on the wings and tail. Immature males start changing to adult plumage from December onwards, and are known by the irregular black spotting on their throats; by April many are seen in this plumage. Of all the sprightly warbler family, none comes nearer to perpetual motion than the redstart. Flying out here, fluttering there, constantly flirting its brightly coloured tail, the only problem it poses to the watcher is that of keeping it in view in his binoculars. Frequents woodland, shrubbery, coppice, etc.

Voice: the song, heard in April from both adult and immature males, consists of two or three different phrases which are repeated or alternated.

BLACKBIRDS and ORIOLES
Icteridae

BOBOLINK *Dolichonyx oryzivorus*   RTP 54

Status: NP: A COMMON, and on certain days an abundant, PASSAGE MIGRANT. The spring passage lasts barely one month, and most birds go through in a rush in the second week of May. The autumn passage is spread over two months, the main body passing in September. Extreme dates: 11 April, 28 May; 27 August*, 12 December*. Out Is: found throughout the Bahamas on migration. Early spring and autumn dates: Gd. Bahama, 9 April, 13 August.

Description, habits: L 7″ The male in spring plumage has the head, wings, and *underparts black*, a *white back*, and a large, creamy-buff patch on the back of the head and neck. Autumn males, and females at all times of year, have yellowish-buff plumage, with dark stripes on the head and upperparts. Spring flocks, with the brightly coloured males mingled with the duller females, are recognised at a glance, but in autumn a closer look is necessary.

Other birds migrate more or less unobtrusively; only Bobolinks come suddenly in large flocks, swarm all over the island, and then in a matter of days are gone, leaving only a few stragglers. The first big spring day ('Bobolink Sunday') usually falls between 8 and 12 May. A flock of Bobolinks may number anything from half a dozen to several hundred birds. They feed on the ground, birds at the back flying up and settling in front of the feeding flock, they walk with swaggering gait, and they fly fast in compact groups. They are commonest on the golf courses and in fields of rough grass, but are also found by roadsides, in wasteland, etc. Passing flocks settle, and perhaps roost, in treetops.

Voice: the flight-note is a distinctive 'quink', often heard from flocks migrating overhead at night. Alarm-note: a harsh 'cherk'. In spring it is quite common for a flock (often settled high in casuarinas) to break into a concert of babbling song, and individual birds will sometimes sing from a bush or sprig.

RED-WINGED BLACKBIRD *Agelaius phoeniceus* Pl 13; RTP 53
Status: NP: COMMON RESIDENT. Out Is: confined to the northern Bahamas (south to Andros and Eleuthera). Also recorded at Cay Sal.
Description, habits: L 8½″ Adult males are *jet-black with scarlet shoulder-patches* or 'epaulets'. Females are less distinctive, being brown with heavily striped underparts, and there is a confusing welter of other plumages; young, immature male, moulting, etc., varying from pale-brown to speckled black and, on males, epaulets varying from yellowish to red. However 'redwings' are noisy, gregarious, swamp-loving birds, and a flock usually contains one or more well-marked individuals. In summer, Red-winged Blackbirds are found distributed across most of the mangrove swamps of the island, but as soon as nesting is over they return to certain favourite marshes. Here they pass the winter in flocks of 30 or more birds, though some perhaps leave the island. On winter evenings they fly to communal roosts, which may be at some distance from their daytime feeding grounds. Though always closely associated with mangroves, 'redwings' will visit quite different habitats when these are close at hand. For instance, they are found among casuarinas and feeding among horses on the south side of Hobby Horse Hall, but would not be found there were it not for the adjacent swamp. In spite of their characteristic noisiness, they are not necessarily conspicuous, as they often perch in the middle of the thickest mangrove, and at other times will be found walking about on the mud, feeding, and in either case can easily be overlooked.
Voice: the song is a loud, grating 'okleeeoo', very distinctive, usually given from a tree, telephone wire, or prominent sprig of mangrove. The common alarm note is a loud 'chek', but there are various other notes: a high, squeaky 'eet', a conversational 'blik, blik', and sundry whistling sounds. From August until late spring, flocks keep up a loud, garbled chattering and attempts at song—'tuning up'—so it is hard to note when the period of real song begins and ends. I think that most of it occurs between March and July.
Nest: a well-made cup of sedge and grasses, placed from 1 to 6 ft. up in mangroves, clumps of rushes, etc. The 3 or 4 eggs (usually 3 in my experience) are pale-bluish, with reddish and purply markings, often including a distinctive 'pencil line' or 'scribbling'. The breeding season is from April to July.

BLACK-COWLED ORIOLE *Icterus dominicensis* (Formerly Bahaman Oriole)   **Pl 11**
Status: NP: not found. Out Is: resident on Andros and Abaco only.
Description: L 8″ s A. A conspicuous *black and yellow* bird, mainly black but with yellow shoulders, rump, and posterior underparts. It is noisy and active and not likely to be confused with other species.

NORTHERN ORIOLE *Icterus galbula* (Formerly Baltimore Oriole)
                                                                                    RTP 54
Status: NP: UNCOMMON PASSAGE MIGRANT. April (8th) to May (7th); September (14th*) to December (14th). Out Is: recorded regularly on Eleuthera, and presumably occurs on all islands on migration.
Description, habits: L 7½″ The male Northern Oriole is an unmistakable medley of *orange and black*, the black head and orange underparts being most noticeable. Females are less brightly coloured and are rather variable, usually with greenish upperparts and orange-yellow underparts; they can be momentarily puzzling. However the two *white wingbars* distinguish them from female tanagers (except Western Tanagers), orioles being further distinguished by their thin, sharp bills, tanagers by their relatively thick and heavy ones. Northern Orioles are perhaps commoner than the records indicate, for they frequent the higher parts of thick, leafy trees, where they are not easily noticed. Their distinctive call, a double-noted whistle, sometimes draws attention to them.

TANAGERS
Thraupidae

STRIPE-HEADED TANAGER *Spindalis zena* (Formerly Bahaman Spindalis)   **Pl 12**
Status: NP: COMMON RESIDENT. Out Is: resident on most main islands.
Description, habits: L 6½″ The *brightly coloured* male plumage is a striking combination of black, white, yellow, orange, and chestnut. Most noticeable are the broad, white lines above and below the eye on the otherwise black head, the white wing-markings, and the intense chestnut patches on the nape and rump. Female plumage, on the other hand, is *entirely nondescript*: greyish-brown, slightly paler on the underparts, with horizontal white edgings on the wings. Adult females have a small, square, white spot on the lower part of the wing—a good field-mark if looked for—and may show a yellowish tinge on the upper breast.

Stripe-headed Tanagers are mostly found among pines and casuarinas during the breeding season, but at other times of year they wander to other types of habitat, notably coppice. They feed principally on berries, but also take the tender tips of leaves and small plants; I have once seen a snail taken, though the bird failed to smash the shell. When not feeding, or when alarmed, they like to perch high in a tree or to fly here and there among well-grown conifers, and consequently they are quite hard to observe.

Voice: the song at the beginning of the season is a weak twittering, but it becomes more vigorous and varied as the summer progresses. Though uninteresting from a distance, it is surprisingly sweet and melodious from close to. Usually sings from a high perch, often the very top of a tree; also in flight, when the male flies from the topmost point of a pine or casuarina, circles round with slowly beating wings, in full song, and then dives down to the same or another perch. See Song Chart, p. 132. There is a lyrical subsong, so soft as to be almost inaudible. The call-note is a loud 'seeip'. Small flocks keep up a soft 'tit-tit-tit' or 'si-si-si', often hard to locate.

Nest: stated to be a small cup in a bush or tree, in which 2 or 3 spotted eggs are laid. Young birds are seen from June onwards.

SUMMER TANAGER *Piranga rubra*   RTP 54

Status: NP: RARE PASSAGE MIGRANT. Some individuals stay for a month or two in autumn, but not all winter. September (20th*) to January (1st). No recent spring records. Out Is: almost no data, but no doubt occurs on passage.

Description: L 7¼″ Adult males have the *entire plumage red.* (The only other mainly red bird is the male Scarlet Tanager (see Appendix), which has black wings and tail.) Females and immatures have uniform, greenish upperparts and orange-yellow underparts, and are distinguished from similar species by the *lack of wingbars* and by the lack of contrast in the wing-colours (blackish on the female Scarlet, nondescript on the present species). Summer Tanagers are found in open woodland, perching in trees and sallying out after insects with rapid, swooping flight.

GROSBEAKS, GRASSQUITS and BUNTINGS
Emberizidae

ROSE-BREASTED GROSBEAK *Pheucticus ludovicianus*   RTP 56
Status: NP: RARE PASSAGE MIGRANT. April (8th); October (3rd*) to
November (9th*). Out Is: seldom recorded, but occurs on migration. Late
spring date: Inagua, 14 April.
Description: L 8" The male in breeding plumage has mainly black upperparts, white underparts, and a *rose-red breast*. Unfortunately males seen
on passage are likely to be changing plumage—enough red colouring
remaining, however, to facilitate identification. Females have drab, brown
upperparts and whitish underparts and are identified by the three *broad
white stripes on the head* (one over each eye, one on the crown) and two
white wingbars. The *heavy, rounded bill* is always distinctive.

BLUE GROSBEAK *Guiraca caerulea*   RTP 56
Status: NP: UNCOMMON PASSAGE MIGRANT. April (17th*) to May (2nd*);
September (1st*) to mid-November*. Out Is: recorded only from Gd.
Bahama, Eleuthera and Harbour Is (late autumn date, 26 November),
but presumably occurs on most islands on migration.
Description, habits: L 7" Male plumage is a uniform *dull-blue* with two
brown wingbars; female and immature plumage (in which this species is
usually seen) is reddish-brown. Blue Grosbeaks could be confused with the
next species but for their larger size and *thick, conical bills*. And see 'Voice'.
Blue Grosbeaks feed unobtrusively in high grass or on the ground, flying
to cover when disturbed. They are found singly or in small groups.
Voice: the usual note is a loud 'spink', similar to the call of a waterthrush.

INDIGO BUNTING *Passerina cyanea*   RTP 56
Status: NP: COMMON WINTER VISITOR. Arrives in the second half of
October, becoming common by the end of the month. Leaves during
April. Extreme dates: 21 September*, 8 May. Out Is: recorded from most,
and no doubt found on all, main islands in winter.
Description, habits: L 5½" The male breeding plumage is of an *intense blue*
colour, but this is replaced in autumn by the same reddish-brown plumage
as is worn by females all year round, though an adult male usually shows
traces of blue on the wings and tail. Males start changing back to breeding
plumage from December onwards, and become a patchwork of blues and

browns until the full dress is attained in April. Females, with their plain brown plumage, are rather similar to female Black-faced Grassquits but are distinguished by their much *redder* colouring—almost rufous on the head. Indigo Buntings are found in small flocks and feed in casuarinas, undergrowth, or long grass, often with grassquits. They are wilder than grassquits, and difficult to approach.

Voice: this is one of the few winter visitors that sings regularly on New Providence, and groups of males often sing together from the same tree. The song is a rambling affair mostly on two notes, descending in cadence. See Song Chart, p. 132. Call-note: 'tzeet', similar to that of the Greater Antillean Bullfinch. Alarm-note: a sharp 'spit'.

PAINTED BUNTING *Passerina ciris*   RTP 56
Status: NP: FAIRLY COMMON PASSAGE MIGRANT, UNCOMMON WINTER VISITOR. Arrives in the second half of October and leaves again in early April. It seems from the St Augustine's Monastery records that migration reaches a peak in November and again in March and early April. Extreme dates: 5 October*; 29 April. Out Is: only recorded from the northern islands. Also seen Exuma (B-B). Presumably occurs throughout the islands on migration. Early date (an exceptional one?): Gd. Bahama, 13 August.
Description, habits: L 5¼″ The adult male Painted Bunting is the most *gaudily coloured* North American bird—an unbelievable mixture of vivid greens, purples, and reds, distributed on the back, head, and underparts respectively. Females and immatures have *plain green* plumage, brighter on the rump and yellower on the underparts, and are our only small, all-green birds.

Similar to Indigo Buntings and Black-faced Grassquits in habits, size, and shape (but not in colour), Painted Buntings feed mostly among long grasses, fluttering up to pull the grass down to earth to get at the seeds. In spite of their bright colours they are easily overlooked; they are very shy, and are fond of shady, overgrown places where they are unlikely to attract attention. They are often found in pairs, or in groups of 3 or 4 birds of which only one is an adult male—perhaps family parties.

GREATER ANTILLEAN BULLFINCH *Loxigilla violacea*   Pl 12
Status: NP: COMMON RESIDENT. Out Is: resident on most main islands.
Description, habits: L 6½″ s A. Adult plumage is *jet-black, with orange-red patches* over the eyes, like eyebrows, on the throat, and under the tail. The heavy bill is also noticeable. Immatures are similar except that the

general colouring is brown. There is also an intermediate (?) smoke-grey plumage, and birds changing from brown or grey to black have irregular patches of the darker colour. At all times, however, the orange-red patches are distinctive. The black adult plumage seems to be acquired very slowly, for there are always many birds in brown plumage and indeed it is so common to see a mixed pair of bullfinches, the male black, the female brown, that I conclude that males do not normally pair or breed until they have acquired adult plumage, whereas females will freely do so in 'immature' plumage.

Bullfinches are typical of coppice, scrub, and thick wooded undergrowth, but are also found in pine woods and in gardens. They feed principally on berries, which they peel, turning them in their beak like parrots; green shoots, buds, and also snails are sometimes taken, though they do not appear to have learnt how to break the shells of the latter. Although common and conspicuously coloured, bullfinches are not often seen, partly because of their choice of habitat and partly because they are unobtrusive, feeding quietly in one place and not moving as one passes. They usually fly only short distances—to the nearest patch of cover—but in flight their stout build and dark colours are distinctive. They are normally found singly or in pairs, except for family groups when the young leave the nest.

Voice: the call-note is a shrill 't'zeet', distinctive except for its resemblance to the note of the Indigo Bunting. Alarm-note: a thin 'spit'. The song is a strained repetition of the call-note: 't'seet, t'seet, tseet, seet, seet, seet, seet, seet', usually given from thick cover. Occasionally a high, exposed branch is chosen, the song then being given both perched and during a butterfly-like flight, but this is unusual. See Song Chart p. 132. Both the song and call-notes are useful guides to the presence of this species.

Nest: builds a substantial, globular nest of twigs and leaves, placed at varying elevations in trees, and is stated to lay 3 spotted eggs. The nesting season seems to be in April and May.

YELLOW-FACED GRASSQUIT *Tiaris olivacea* Pl 12

Status: NP: resident, introduced in 1963. Out Is: not found.

Description, habits: L 4½″ The male is identified by the *bright yellow stripe* over each eye, *square-cut yellow throat*, and black breast. The remaining plumage is dull olive, paler on the underparts. Females are more poorly marked, but retain a suggestion of the face pattern and some traces of yellow. Habits and habitat similar to following species.

Accidentally introduced in small numbers (see Melodious Grassquit for circumstances), the Yellow-faced Grassquit is reported, in 1966, to have established itself in at least two locations on New Providence.

BLACK-FACED GRASSQUIT *Tiaris bicolor* Pl 12

Status: NP: ABUNDANT RESIDENT. Out Is: a common resident on almost all islands.

Description, habits: L 4½″ Adult males have dark-olive upperparts and *black heads and underparts*; females and immatures have dull olive-brown upperparts and paler underparts. The plumage of either sex is entirely lacking in stripes, spots, yellow markings, or other distinguishing features, but the males can hardly be confused with any other species. These abundant and tame little birds are often overlooked on account of their small size, sober plumage, and unobtrusive habits. They are widely distributed, being found in gardens, fields, woodland, scrub, undergrowth, and by roadsides.

Their food is principally grass seeds, although they feed high in casuarinas when the seeds of that tree are ripe, and sometimes take berries. It is amusing to watch grassquits feeding, for they often flutter up to catch a long grass in their beak, pull it to earth, and proceed to eat the seeds in the manner of man eating a corn-cob. At other times they deliberately perch on a grass-stem too weak to hold their weight, and come swaying triumphantly to earth with it. They are sociable birds, being found in pairs and small groups even during the breeding season. In winter they join forces with flocks of Indigo Buntings, never, however, flocking in such numbers as the buntings.

The population of Black-faced Grassquits on New Providence may be adversely affected by the recent introduction of Yellow-faced and Melodious Grassquits.

Voice: the song is a pleasant, though monotonous 'tink tink tink tseeeee'. From July onwards the young, still in immature plumage, imitate their elders with infinite variations and abbreviations. The song is usually delivered from medium height in a tree or bush, sometimes from the ground. See Song Chart, p. 132. The call-note is a soft 'teep'; the alarm, chiefly heard when nest or young are near, is a short, emphatic 'chip', sometimes extended to a louder 'fitchick'.

Nest: builds a relatively large, poorly constructed, domed nest of grasses, with the entrance in the side, rather like a large, loosely made bananaquit's nest. When placed in a tree or bush, the nest rests on a horizontal branch, whereas bananaquits usually choose forks in vertical branches. The few nests that I have found have been from 2 to 5 ft. up, either on low branches or well concealed in clumps of reeds or coarse grass. In either case they shared the unusual characteristic, for such an essentially land-dwelling bird, of being over water. Grassquits no doubt also nest high in pines or casuarinas and perhaps on the ground, but I have not seen nests in these situations. The usual clutch is 2 eggs, sometimes 3; they are white with reddish-brown spots, zoned round the thick end. The breeding season extends from February to October, April and May being the busiest months.

MELODIOUS GRASSQUIT *Tiaris canora* (Other name: Cuban Grass-quit) **Pl 12**
Status: NP: resident, introduced in 1963. See below. Out Is: not found.
Description: habits: L 4½″ The male is identified by its *black face*, framed by a horseshoe-shaped, *bright yellow collar*. The upperparts are olive-green, the underparts greyish with a black area on the breast. Females have a similar pattern, but the colours are less bright and the black is lacking, being replaced by grey and rust-coloured on the face. Habitat and habits similar to preceding species.

An aeroplane carrying a consignment of 600 'Cuban finches' from Cuba to a zoo in Europe made an emergency landing in Nassau in March 1963, and about 200 birds died as a result of the unexpected delay. Most of the rest were freed on New Providence, and it is estimated that about 300 were Melodious Grassquits (there were a few Indigo Buntings, Yellow-faced Grassquits, and possibly other species in the consignment). The freed birds dispersed very quickly and virtually disappeared within a year, but subsequently recovered and established themselves as a breeding species. Reported, in 1966, as fairly common in Nassau and eastern New Providence.

DICKCISSEL *Spiza americana* **RTP 56**
Status: NP: RARE PASSAGE MIGRANT. September (3rd*) to October (19th*). Out Is: recorded only from Gd. Bahama (late date: 23 November) and Inagua, but no doubt occurs on most islands on migration.
Description: L 6¼″ A sparrow-like bird identified by its yellow breast-markings, yellow stripe over the eye, and chestnut shoulder-mark, though these are more or less noticeable according to age and sex. Adult males may show traces of black on their throats. Occurs among Bobolink flocks.

SAVANNAH SPARROW *Passerculus sandwichensis*   RTP 57
Status: NP: UNCOMMON WINTER VISITOR. October (11th*) to April (25th*). Out Is: recorded from the northern Bahamas (south to Rum Cay) in winter. Common round Hatchet Bay, Eleuthera.
Description, habits: L 5¾″ s A. Savannah Sparrows have rich-brown upperparts with dark streakings, and white *underparts with heavy, dark streaks.* There are three yellowish stripes on the head—one over each eye and one on the crown—and the tail is slightly forked. Found only in a few areas on New Providence (e.g. St Augustine's Monastery farm and Lyford Cay), Savannah Sparrows occur in flocks of up to about 20 birds. They live among long grasses and tangled weeds, feeding on the ground and escaping detection by running. When flushed they fly a short distance and drop into the grass again, but if flushed several times they fly to some nearby perch, where they can be well seen.

GRASSHOPPER SPARROW *Ammodramus savannarum*   RTP 57
Status: NP: UNCOMMON WINTER VISITOR. October (12th*) to May (1st). Out Is: recorded in winter from the northern Bahamas (south to San Salvador).
Description, habits: L 5″ s A. A small sparrow with pale, *unstreaked underparts* and a short, pointed tail. The upperparts are brown with light streaks, the underparts a plain, clear buffish colour. There is a pale streak, bordered by two darker ones, along the crown, and a yellowish mark between the eye and the bill. The Grasshopper closely resembles the Savannah Sparrow in general habits, and the two species are likely to be found together. The Grasshopper is still more difficult to flush than the other, and is seldom seen.

CLAY-COLOURED SPARROW *Spizella pallida*   RTP 58
Status: NP: RARE WINTER VISITOR. October (25th*) to February (13th*). Out Is: not recorded, but no doubt occurs in winter in the northern Bahamas.
Description: L 5½″ s A. The clear, unmarked breast, striped head, and *dark cheek-patch* identify this sparrow, which has only been recorded from the region of St Augustine's Monastery.

WHITE-CROWNED SPARROW *Zonotrichia leucophrys*   RTP 58
Status: NP: RARE PASSAGE MIGRANT. October (4th*) to November

(24th). Out Is: recorded only from Bimini and Gd. Bahama (late date: 26 November), but is to be expected on most islands on passage.

Description: L 7″ s A. Adults have a broad, white stripe on the centre of the crown, bordered by black stripes and then again white ones. Usually seen in immature plumage, with *rufous and buff head-stripes* instead of the more distinctive black and white ones. The back is brown with dark markings, as with other sparrows, but the unstreaked, greyish-brown underparts and pale bill are helpful points.

APPENDIX 1

ACCIDENTALS

The following species are of occasional occurrence in the Bahamas, and none of them has been recorded on New Providence more than twice in recent years. Dates of occurrence and *presumed* status are shown. My own records are marked §.

CORY'S SHEARWATER (*Puffinus diomedea*) ⎤ Reported, and to be expected
GREATER SHEARWATER (*Puffinus gravis*) ⎬ occasionally, in Bahamian
SOOTY SHEARWATER (*Puffinus griseus*) ⎦ waters.

WHITE PELICAN (*Pelecanus erythrorhynchos*) Bimini 4–8 March, Joulter's Cay (N. Andros) 11 June: vagrant from Florida.

GREAT WHITE HERON (*Ardea occidentalis*) Recorded from Andros: vagrant from Florida.

WOOD STORK (*Mycteria americana*) Gd. Bahama 25 October 1964: vagrant from Florida.

FULVOUS TREE DUCK (*Dendrocygna bicolor*) NP 22 December§–1 January: also Gd. Bahama (17 & 25 October, 12 & 14 November), Exuma and Inagua: occasional winter visitor.

GADWALL (*Anas strepera*) NP 19–26 January 1963§: occasional winter visitor.

REDHEAD (*Aythya americana*) Stated to have been the most abundant duck on NP in 1859: no recent records: to be looked for in winter.

RED-BREASTED MERGANSER (*Mergus serrator*) Recorded NP: occasional winter visitor.

BLACK RAIL (*Laterallus jamaicensis*) Eleuthera October 1954: occasional migrant or winter visitor.

LAPWING (*Vanellus vanellus*) An old record from Paradise Is: a stray from Europe.

RED KNOT (*Calidris canutus*) Harbour Is 11 November 1961: occasional passage migrant.

BUFF-BREASTED SANDPIPER (*Tryngites subruficollis*) NP 24 September 1961§: occasional vagrant after hurricanes.

HUDSONIAN GODWIT (*Limosa haemastica*) Eleuthera 5 November 1961: autumn vagrant (normally migrates out to sea).

NORTHERN PHALAROPE (*Lobipes lobatus*) NP 11–12 October 1959§: also either this or Wilson's Phalarope, Little Exuma 3 April§: occasional passage migrant.

PARASITIC JAEGER (*Stercorarius parasiticus*)⎫ Known to occur in Bahamian
POMARINE JAEGER (*Stercorarius pomarinus*) ⎭ waters in winter.

BONAPARTE'S GULL (*Larus philadelphia*) NP 7-20 March§: also Gd. Bahama late December, and Long Is 8 October: vagrant after storms.

FORSTER'S TERN (*Sterna forsteri*) Exuma 21 November 1954: occasional winter vagrant.

CASPIAN TERN (*Hydroprogne caspia*) Inagua 10 April 1961: vagrant from Florida.

DOVEKIE (*Plautus alle*) Gd. Bahama 7 December 1962 (an oiled bird): winter vagrant.

CHIMNEY SWIFT (*Chaetura pelagica*) NP 1 May§, 23 August§, also Eleuthera 16 April, 23 October: occasional passage migrant.

RUBY-THROATED HUMMINGBIRD (*Archilochus colubris*) An old winter record from NP: Gd. Bahama 22–25 November: occasional winter visitor.

RUFOUS HUMMINGBIRD (*Selasphorus rufus*) Gd. Bahama 20 October 1966: winter vagrant.

FERNANDINA'S FLICKER (*Nesoceleus fernandinae*) Gd. Bahama 16 October 1964: accidental stray: a Cuban species presumed displaced by hurricane 'Isabel'.

GIANT KINGBIRD (*Tyrannus cubensis*) Recorded from Gt. Inagua, where a rare vagrant.

SCISSOR-TAILED FLYCATCHER (*Muscivora forficata*) Gd. Bahama 31 October 1964: winter vagrant.

GREAT CRESTED FLYCATCHER (*Myiarchus crinitus*) NP 14 October, also Eleuthera: occasional passage migrant.

EASTERN PHOEBE (*Sayornis phoebe*) Bimini 18 November, Gd. Bahama 10 October: occasional winter visitor.

EASTERN WOOD PEWEE (*Contopus virens*) NP 19 & 20 October in different years: also Gd. Bahama and Eleuthera (15 October to 1 November): occasional passage migrant.

HOUSE WREN (*Troglodytes aedon*) NP 23 November 1967. Bimini 18-19 November 1962, Exuma late February: occasional winter visitor.

BROWN THRASHER (*Toxostoma rufum*) Gd. Bahama 29 September and 16 October (in different years), Harbour Is 28 November: almost certainly seen NP 10 January§: winter vagrant.

AMERICAN ROBIN (*Turdus migratorius*) NP 25 December: also Bimini, Gd. Bahama, and Eleuthera: occasional winter visitor.

WOOD THRUSH (*Hylocichla mustelina*) NP 15 April§ and previously re-

corded: also Gd. Bahama 10 October, 13 November, and Cay
Lobos: occasional passage migrant.

HERMIT THRUSH (*Hylocichla guttata*) NP 6 November, Gd. Bahama 15, 17,
& 25 November (in different years): occasional winter visitor.

VEERY (*Hylocichla fuscescens*) NP 1 May 1960§: also Cay Lobos: occasional passage migrant.

RUBY-CROWNED KINGLET (*Regulus calendula*) NP regularly from 7 November 1960§ to 4 March 1961§, Gd. Bahama 17 November
1960: evidently a small 'wave' that year: also Gd. Bahama
November 1963: occasional winter visitor.

CEDAR WAXWING (*Bombycilla cedrorum*) NP an old March record: recent
records from Gd. Bahama (14 October – 17 November) and
Eleuthera: an old April record from Berry Is: occasional winter
visitor.

WATER PIPIT (*Anthus spinoletta*) NP 13§ December, 14§ January (in different winters): also Gd. Bahama (November, December and
February) and, possibly, Green Cay: occasional winter visitor.

SPRAGUE'S PIPIT (*Anthus spragueii*) Gd. Bahama 19–23 October 1966:
winter vagrant.

LOGGERHEAD SHRIKE (*Lanius ludovicianus*) Collected on Andros by Neville
Chamberlain; recorded Gd. Bahama 10 October 1964: winter
vagrant.

SOLITARY VIREO (*Vireo solitarius*) NP 18 November, Harbour Is 25–28
November (in different years), and Eleuthera in April: occasional
passage migrant.

PHILADELPHIA VIREO (*Vireo philadelphicus*) NP 29 October 1960, Eleuthera
31 October 1961: occasional passage migrant.

SWAINSON'S WARBLER (*Limnothlypis swainsonii*) NP 19 September: 2 or 3
records from Out Is: occasional passage migrant.

GOLDEN-WINGED WARBLER (*Vermivora chrysoptera*) NP 22 September§,
14 October (both 1962): also Eleuthera: occasional passage
migrant.

BACHMAN'S WARBLER (*Vermivora bachmanii*) Recorded, Cay Sal, on migration: not to be expected elsewhere.

ORANGE-CROWNED WARBLER (*Vermivora celata*) NP 21 October, 22
November: also Gd. Bahama, Abaco, Eleuthera, and San
Salvador (14 October to 1 January): occasional winter visitor.

CERULEAN WARBLER (*Dendroica cerulea*) NP 17–18 September, 18 October.
Also Cay Lobos. Occasional passage migrant.

MOURNING WARBLER (*Oporornis philadelphia*) NP 23 September 1960,
23 September 1962§: occasional passage migrant.

YELLOW-BREASTED CHAT (*Icteria virens*) Bimini and Gd. Bahama 16–17

August and 17–22 November: occasional winter visitor.

WILSON'S WARBLER (*Wilsonia pusilla*) NP 17 & 24 September 1961, Gd. Bahama 9 April: occasional passage migrant.

HOUSE SPARROW (*Passer domesticus*) Nassau June 1959§, May 1960§, Gd. Bahama 12 & 14 November 1964 and 14 November 1965: Probably strays brought over by ship from Florida. Unsuccessfully introduced in Nassau in the 1870s.

YELLOW-HEADED BLACKBIRD (*Xanthocephalus xanthocephalus*) Gd. Bahama 16 October 1965: winter vagrant.

ORCHARD ORIOLE (*Icterus spurius*) Eleuthera May: occasional passage migrant.

RUSTY BLACKBIRD (*Euphagus carolinus*) Gd. Bahama 20 October 1967: winter vagrant.

BREWER'S BLACKBIRD (*Euphagus cyanocephalus*) Gd. Bahama 13 November 1959: occasional winter visitor.

BROWN-HEADED COWBIRD (*Molothrus ater*) NP 4 October and mid-February: occasional winter visitor.

WESTERN TANAGER (*Piranga ludoviciana*) NP 11 & 26§ September: occasional passage migrant.

SCARLET TANAGER (*Piranga olivacea*) NP 18 April, 29–30 September§: also Andros and Cay Lobos: occasional passage migrant.

AMERICAN GOLDFINCH (*Spinus tristis*) Gd. Bahama 15 October to 11 April: occasional winter visitor.

VESPER SPARROW (*Pooecetes gramineus*) Gd. Bahama 15 November and late December: occasional winter visitor.

LARK SPARROW (*Chondestes grammacus*) NP 11 September to 1 October: also Bimini and Gd. Bahama in August: occasional passage migrant.

DARK-EYED JUNCO (*Junco hyemalis*) NP 18 November 1959: occasional winter visitor.

CHIPPING SPARROW (*Spizella passerina*) NP 16 January, Gd. Bahama 13 & 18 November, in different years: Harbour Is 24–25 November: occasional winter visitor.

LINCOLN'S SPARROW (*Melospiza lincolnii*) Gd. Bahama 20 October: Abaco, 11 November: Harbour Is 24–26 November (in different years): occasional winter visitor.

SWAMP SPARROW (*Melospiza georgiana*) NP 10 & 18 November, Mayaguana 10 April: occasional passage migrant.

SONG SPARROW (*Melospiza melodia*) Recorded once NP; also Gd. Bahama: occasional winter visitor.

SNOW BUNTING (*Plectrophenax nivalis*) Cat Is 1 December 1963: winter vagrant.

APPENDIX 2:
SONG CHART OF SOME COMMON SONGBIRDS
(New Providence)

APPENDIX 2: SONG CHART OF SOME COMMON SONGBIRDS
(New Providence)

	JAN	FEB	MAR	APR
NORTHERN MOCKINGBIRD	 xxxxxxxxXXXXXXXXXX			
RED-LEGGED THRUSH	x			
THICK-BILLED VIREO	xxxxxxxXXXXXXXXXXX			
BLACK-WHISKERED VIREO				AX
BANANAQUIT	. . . . x x x xXXXXXXXXXX			
STRIPE-HEADED TANAGER	. . . . .x x x			
INDIGO BUNTING	 xxxxxxxxxXXX			
GR. ANTILLEAN BULLFINCH	. . . . .x x x			
BLACK-FACED GRASSQUIT	xxxxxxXXXXXXXXXXXX			

KEY	. . . .	*infrequent song, subsong, etc.*
	xxxxxxxxxxxx	*regular song*
	XXXXXXX	*constant song*
A ARRIVES		L LEAVES

MAY	JUNE	JULY	AUG	SEPT	OCT	NOV	DEC

XXXXXXXXXXXXXXXxxx. . . . . .XXXXXXXX . . . .

xxXXXXXXXXXXXXXXXxxxxx . . . . .

Xxxxxxxxxxxxxxxxx . . . .

XXXXXXXXXXXXXXXXxxx   L

XXxxxxxxxxxxxx . . . .

xXXXXXXXXXXXXXxxxxxxxxxxx . . . .

L   A . . . .

xXXXXXXXXXxxxxxxxxxxxxxx . . . .

XXXxxxxxxx . . . .

Index

Figures in **bold** type refer to plates on which birds appear

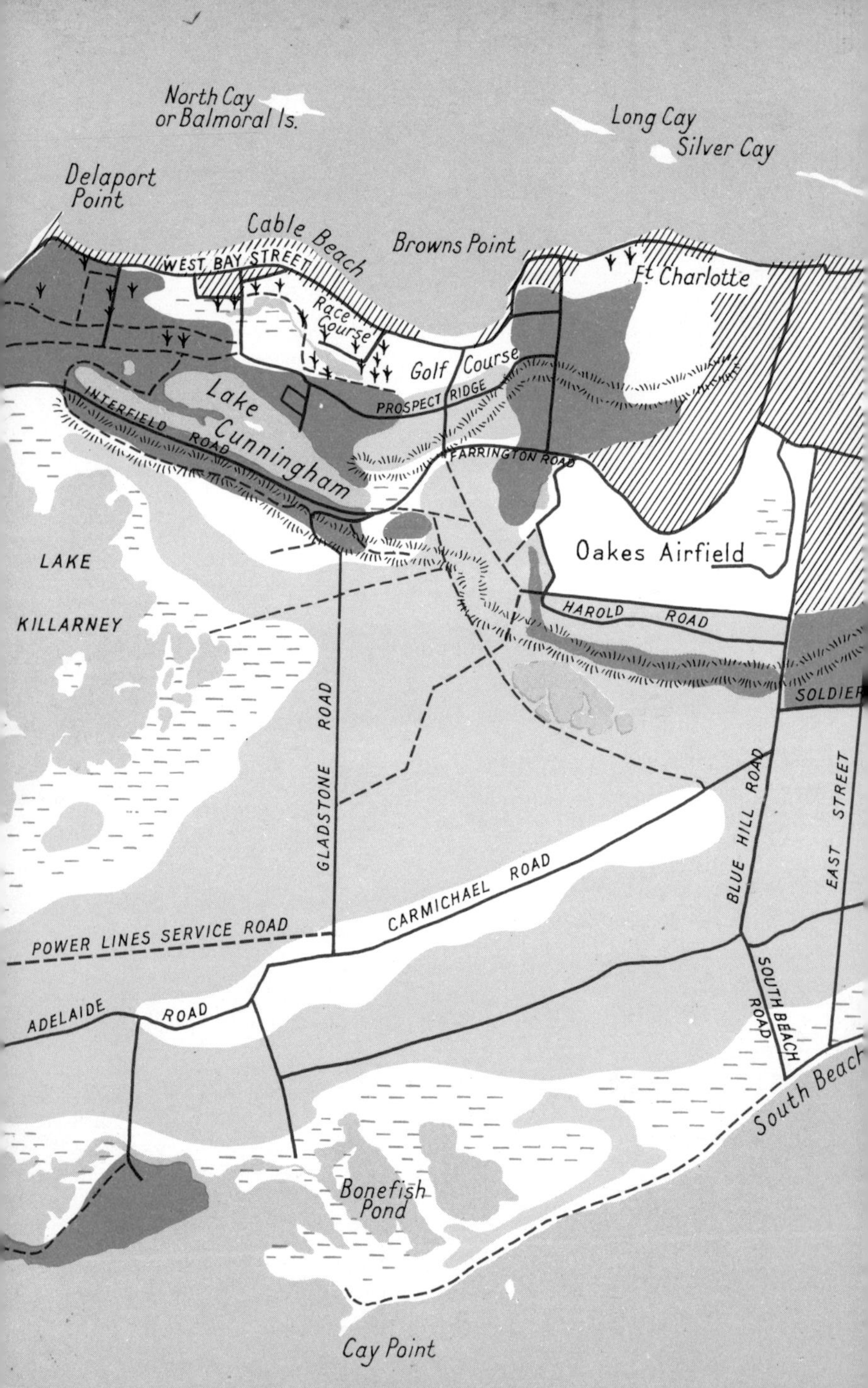

North Cay
or Balmoral Is.
Long Cay
Silver Cay
Delaport
Point
Cable Beach
Browns Point
WEST BAY STREET
Ft Charlotte
Race
Course
Golf Course
PROSPECT RIDGE
Lake
Cunningham
INTERFIELD
ROAD
FARRINGTON ROAD
Oakes Airfield
LAKE
KILLARNEY
HAROLD ROAD
SOLDIER
GLADSTONE ROAD
BLUE HILL ROAD
EAST STREET
CARMICHAEL ROAD
POWER LINES SERVICE ROAD
ADELAIDE ROAD
SOUTH BEACH ROAD
South Beach
Bonefish
Pond
Cay Point